For my buddy
Merle —

Steve Buchman

1059 S.
Hayworth

There are no real people in this book.
I of course took elements of many people
for the writing of it, but any identification
of actual persons is strictly coincidental.

Stephen Bindman, PhD

Love
Without
Illusions

By
Stephen Bindman, Ph.D.

First Edition
Printed in the United States of America
Typeset by Delmas Typesetting, Ann Arbor, MI

Published by: Human Futures
                P.O. Box 893
                Hermosa Beach, CA 90254

Library of Congress Catalog Card Number 85-080019

ISBN 0-932385-19-2

To all realists who have not abandoned the pleasures of companionship, intimacy and joy

Table of Contents

Introduction

As I write this, I am imagining you, my potential reader, picking this book up late on a Saturday afternoon, alone, aware that you are without a partner to spend time with this evening that is a special time for couples, for dating. Like many other people, you find these are confusing, difficult times for love relationships. Perhaps your eye passes to a nearby magazine; the magazines are full of articles on relationships. An issue of Los Angeles Magazine that I noticed as I wrote this chapter had an interview with a panel of women on "What's Wrong with Los Angeles Men."

Such an approach is more tempting to some than mine in this book. An important focus of this book is understanding your contribution to your not being in a relationship, not what is the matter with everyone else. I hope you will learn to understand your own functioning, how you get into relationships, how you get out of them, how you make your relationships what they are for you. Change is always difficult. It is still easier to change yourself than others.

Most people I have heard discuss our current problems with love relationships have a focus outside themselves. They prefer to make remarks like the following:

"This city has no eligible men."

"Women are such gold-diggers these days."

"I can't find anyone who seems interested in me."

"The only place there seems to be to find anyone is in a bar, and a woman like me who doesn't want to screw around doesn't belong there."

"I can't seem to find a woman who really wants children. I went out with one who was a nursery school teacher, but she seemed scared to death of me."

"I know all the men my age around this university (of 40,000), I'm really thinking of moving."

"Men just want to get in your pants."

"Women—what ever do they want!"

In this book, which is not only for people who are without a relationship but also for those who are stuck at some unworkable point within a relationship, I hope to go beyond such self-protective stories. By vocation, I am a psychotherapist, a clinical psychologist, and this book is based on my experiences with my patients as well as that fund of knowledge that we all collect from our education and experience of life. Some of my patients are seen in these pages in disguised form; I have hidden their identities without changing whatever is important to the point I am making at the moment.

The culture in the advanced industrial countries is on the brink of great changes in personal relationships. Recently there has been some pulling back from the implications of current developments in relationships. Our fear of the changes rising out of new freedoms in social life is behind the apparent return to traditional values, fashions of the past, and nostalgia for the post WWII period. In the west, as in Iran, the new personal freedom made possible by a higher material standard of living, birth control, and widespread dissemination of disparate knowledge is frightening.

We don't have a framework for heterosexual relationships; thus we are turning backwards for the moment as we blind ourselves to the inadequacy of traditional arrangements to our current situation. Actually we are handling relationships in a non-traditional way, since living together, abortion, and pre-marital sex are not traditional solutions, and are widespread. The weaknesses of traditional solutions are most obvious to singles in the advanced industrial countries, and is part of the reason for the change in the nature of marriage and the growth of "living together."

The impossibility of contemporary social life for many people is illustrated in the movies. We have movies where the most extravagant fantasies of scientific advance accompany very traditional personal arrange-ments. On the other hand, there are extraordinarily poignant films like *Tender Mercies*. In this film, there is nothing between the most traditional arrangements, and virtues, on the one hand—contrasted with decadence, drunkenness, death and disorder on the other. A generation ago, the biblical words "There is nothing new under the sun," were still used in the technological sphere, despite the new wonders and dangers science had brought us. We must face now a social life with new realities, and the same biological equipment we have had for thousands of years.

This book is designed for those people who are willing to look rationally and face the truth about one of the most mystified areas of human existence: the truth about our love lives. It is very far from the last word on the subject. It is really only a primer; but my goal has been to tell the truth as I have learned it from my patients, my friends, and my own life. I have no special point of view, or ax to grind, beyond the idea that one of the worst sins is to mislead the young. The truth, even when painful, will give any reader a better place to stand as he constructs the love relationships that we all need. I have included some data on taboo subjects except for homosexuality. My data in that area has been too limited for me too speak comfortably as an expert.

This book is designed for those with some experience of love relationships. It is not particularly for those innocent of experience. Easy reading of this book probably requires at least one important prior love relationship; or as some would say, at least one important failed or ended love affair. To me, no love relationship, no matter how brief, ought to be seen as a failure. That issue, however, is better taken up in the body of the book.

One of the great problems in the area of love relations is that we frequently start out thinking in ready made categories. We use these categories almost automatically. I have chosen examples that may seem unusual or even bizarre, partially to break up your ordinary thinking and free your mind to face reality as it is.

The order of the chapters in this book was made for an imaginary reader: a single person wandering through a bookstore on a Saturday afternoon, with nothing special planned for the evening. If you fit, begin the book at the beginning. Otherwise feel free to pick up the chapters that interest you and forget the rest. Chapter Two has some important general concepts.

1
Starting Over

The first step in creating a love relationship for yourself is facing your own hesitation, despair and fear about relationships. It is quite common for me to hear my patients change radically in their ability to connect with someone new once they have worked through their own feelings about their last relationship.

It took me a long time to discover this, I too was blinded by people's excuses about their difficulties in starting over. Not that it is an easy task; to start over. But the lack of a relationship is almost always due to a withdrawal. This avoidance comes out of their pain and fear from recent loss. I probably learned the importance of recent loss most dramatically from Karl, whose childhood had been tremendously harsh. He won my sympathy quickly. He had never known his father, and his mother had been shot and killed by one of her numerous lovers. Adopted by the judge who had tried his mother's murderer, he was too rebellious to stay long in that pious Christian household. When I met him he had no career and worked at odd jobs. He survived on a small government pension. At that time Karl had no intimate relationships.

It was easy to believe that this was a result of his generally disorganized and fractured life, until one day he began talking to me about his last important girl friend. It soon became clear to me that he was absolutely broken up by the way this rather beautiful and intelligent woman had dropped him because she believed, correctly, that he was fooling around with other women. At that time, his life had been fuller, he had been working, and generally functioning well. After a half-dozen hours dealing with his pain and distress about her "betrayal", his ambivalence towards new women lessened.

I was soon startled to discover that he had a new and substantial relationship. He began living with his new girl friend shortly afterwards. Although Karl still had numerous work problems, he now had a substantial relationship. His case makes it clear that the distant past is not what keeps people out of relationships. The distant past may influence the kind of relationships we create; what is incapacitating for most people are feelings of sadness, anger, and despair about more recent life experiences.

Recent failure and disappointment was central to Fran, a plump woman in early middle age. Like Karl, she had apparently hidden her feelings about those events. She came to see me for help with her adolescent sons who were quite rebellious. Following my usual practice, I saw her as well, and our interviews quickly turned to her own life and its dissatisfactions. Chief amongst these was her lack of a mate. She more than most women was absolutely certain that her life's problems would be solved through marriage. Extremely religious she also claimed to be quite passionate. Like many passionate people Fran disliked casual relationships, and abhorred the bar scene. The vulnerability and openness required for a deep sexual connection do not easily fit into such settings.

She was was either unwilling or unable to meet men in other ways. She supported her children on welfare, and she was no raving beauty. In short, Fran was not what one thinks of as an exciting marriage prospect. Statistically her chances of remarriage looked low.

One day I lost my temper with her concerning her absolute conviction that marriage would rescue her from life's problems. I told her that if marriage was so damned important to her I would see to it that she would ge married shortly, even if she insisted on staying fat.

"You won't play any social games by the rules, that's what keeps you single and that's what you want. Being fat is a great disadvantage in this culture, (as opposed to Libya and the South Pacific where fat women are greatly in demand.) If you really want to get married, at least you ought to lose some weight." She ran out of my office crying and sat weeping on a terrace near my front door.

We reconciled and continued to work after that incident. Suddenly she was losing weight. I had her buy an ad in one of the newspapers that cater to singles who really want to marry. She began to get responses. "I'm only losing this weight because you made me so mad," she said.

What happened next was an amazing lesson to me. As soon as she became serious, and not ambivalent about finding a husband, out of the woodwork crept her old boyfriend of many years who never had been interested in marrying her. She hadn't even bothered mentioning him to me. A former "roomer" who wasn't serious, he had broken up with her not too long before she sought my help. Her feelings were tied to Timmy much more than she wanted to admit. He even had paid for her ad in the singles magazine as an old friend. This ad led to a marriage proposal from a man that Fran liked. Timmy begged and pleaded with her to marry him instead. It soon became clear that Fran had strong feelings for Timmy. That unacknowledged relationship had been very important to her, and she accepted Timmy's proposal.

Fran had many excuses for not finding someone to marry, as did Timmy. Central for both of them were their unacknowledged feelings about each other. They were still importantly attached to each other. They didn't have a good explanation for their attachment, and when their relationship apparently ended, they both acted as if it was unimportant. Not facing her feelings for Timmy, avoiding dealing with her grief and sadness over the end of that relatonship, Fran was really unable to move on. When I managed to finally puncture some of her defenses and she made herself approachable, she got the proposals she said she wanted.

Attitude and seriousness were crucial in Fran's attracting interest to her. Her supposed disadvantages, making her relatively ineligible by some ordinary criteria, were much less important. Once Fran became serious she had to choose between proposals. Survey data on the characteristics of women who marry agree with Fran's experience. It certainly is not necessarily the woman who has the biggest total of marketable qualities.

Carol, the young part time secretary to a colleague, returned after a year in Europe. For months I heard Carol complain of the fact that there was simply no one interested in her. She had had a steady boyfriend since her junior year in high school. Now a part time student, she complained bitterly and piteously of life in Los Angeles. "Los Angeles is the worst city in the world if you're not a winner. If you're old or a bit seedy, no one will even say hello to you!"

This young lady was unceremoniously dumped by her last boy friend. He had been her buddy, her chum, first her brother's pal, then her close friend. When she returned from Europe, she began to date him in a more grown-up fashion. He dumped her unceremoniously after she had given herself to him at last. In this case, for another young lady with a rich father. An abandonment of this sort, not apparently based on anything that Carol had done, was very devastating to her sense of trust and power in a relationship.

For the next six months she complained of her loneliness, of her need to lose weight. She was overweight, but men would accost her at bus stops and on the street nonetheless.

One day, lonely and unable to cope, she broke down and called Betty, another girl friend. Betty rushed over and comforted her for several days. They had many intimate talks. In the process her girl friend discovered Carol's brief liaison, and her painful feelings about its end and her "betrayal". In her friend's loving company she could acknowledge her bitterness and pain more freely. After considerable crying and most important, facing her own subtle ways of withdrawing, her life changed. Within days of that therapeutic experience,

Carol managed to have three dates—without moving from Los Angeles.

One last relevant history comes to my mind. A young English architecture student, an immigrant, had come to see me for help with his sexual problems. A student in his late twenties, he had had only one troublesome love affair a few years previously. That brief dance in his otherwise pedestrian life had developed out of his experience as a roomer with a young couple early in college. He became close to both husband and wife in a casual and relaxed atmosphere. The wife, Judy, was able to understand and see him in ways that his shyness generally hid from others. At a difficult moment in her marriage Judy became his lover. This stirred up great controversy and my patient ended up losing both his circle of friends and his married lover, who returned to her husband. Deeply wounded by this experience, he changed countries and schools, and had no further intimate relationships.

We spent many hours in therapy together dealing slowly with this and that. Eddie remained shy. He got very angry at his mother, and refused to even write her for some time. His relationships with women changed little. Eddie seemed afraid of his sexual inadequacy and he felt he needed a sex surrogate to get started again. He found such a lady, who treated him with some sensitivity for ten sessions. Ed tried to continue the relationship but she refused, out of concern that his attachment to her under the circumstances was excessive.

One day he attended an open seminar of mine. Afterwards I overheard a young teacher say to him "You remind me of my brother." That remark usually indicates a combination of affection and dismissal. Wondering what about Ed had stimulated the dismissal, I looked at Ed through her eyes at that moment. Long and thin, with a wispy beard and unfashionable clothes, there was an air of puppylike neediness that I could see would not appeal to most women serious about connecting for a relationship.

At our next session I gave him a hard time about his beard. "I'm convinced that there's something about the way you present yourself that puts women off. Your beard for instance. I nag at you about it. You pay me this money that is precious to you. It seems to me that if you were serious about connecting with a woman you would at least take my advice about that damn wispy beard...." Ed came in the following week without a beard, his hair trim, and two weeks later he had a girl friend.

One way to digest this experience would be to fit the recommendations of the fashion magazines as well as the toothpaste ads. Yet, there are plenty of people who aren't fashion plates who have relationships. His dress was a political act, a put off, a message like Fran's fat; he wasn't in the dating world.

Once his defenses were punctured, he represented himself in a different way. His decision to dress differently was a decision to be different. Once he had made that shift, it is probably true that how he dressed became much less important. His inner light showed a different hue to the world.

Out of these experiences, and many similar ones, certain things are now clear to me. What keeps people out of love relationships is within them. Something internal accounts for or causes their withdrawal. Most of the time, relatively recent and painful experience is at the root of this withdrawal. The balance of forces that made these patients of mine withdraw needed to shift. That shift in consciousness was absolutely necessary before they could begin to build what they wanted.

Changing your consciousness is not easy. Telling yourself to "be different" won't make the shift. Facing the reasons you have withdrawn, incorporating your fears into your conscious self will help. Ventilating your feelings and acknowledging your loss is important. Time helps a little, but if you do nothing in that time, your hurt will remain insulated and protected from the healing force of new friendships. Openly acknowledge your pain and disappointment. Try to face what went "wrong."

In this book you will find many ideas and ways to digest and understand your experience. Hopefully, in these ways you can free yourself enough from your recent past to be once again intimately involved, perhaps in more workable ways.

Questions To Ask Yourself

Writing down the answers to these questions is a good way to learn to know yourself more. Write them down, and then put the answers away for a few days and look at your answers again. If you wish, you can record your answers on a tape player and listen to them again.

1. What do I like best about being alone? (You're not allowed to say "Nothing.")

2. What was most painful about the end of my last relationship. In what way do I think it can happen again?

3. What was most painful about the end of my best relationship? In what way do I think it can happen again?

2
Finding Someone New

More rationalizing seems to go on about topic this than any other. Most of the self-deceiving tales I hear are of one of two forms. The first kind is, "I can't find the person I want because I'm too ...." (Take your choice of the next word: poor, fat, thin, ugly, tall, short, dramatic looking or sincere.)

The second tale we often tell ourselves has the form, "There seem to be no ..." (Here the choices are among phrases like sensitive men, truly sexy women, men who are serious, women who aren't gold-diggers, unattached women in Anchorage Alaska, etc.)

Rationalizations are interesting statements. Generally they are true statements, that are just not to the point. They are arguments we make to ourselves that allow us to continue doing whatever we have been doing, without looking stupid to ourselves and others. While self deceptions allow us to feel momentarily better about ourselves, and certainly there are moments when that is necessary, they provide poor maps of the world to lead us out of our quandaries.

The logical problem with the first rationalization is clear: There are many poor, thin, fat, ugly, sincere people who have relationships. No single, and few multiple, handicaps seem to prevent people from finding others with whom they can form relationships. A strikingly unusual couple comes to mind about this issue. I once met a rather obese women who had married a struggling young professional man. After a couple of years in this relationship, she decided that she wanted more sexually. Matilda then insisted that her husband accept her taking a lover for herself into their household! So much for handicaps.

When you have low self-esteem it is hard to have the confidence to try for what you want - or trust its presence when you have it. The famous remark of Groucho Marx seems appropriate here: "Any club that would have me, I wouldn't want to join."

Very likely you will find what you want, if you have the courage to seek it out; although it is possible to be so specific in your needs that there are very few people to choose from. Even more destructive is the romantic fantasy that there is only one person for you. Perhaps this was true about your need for your mother when you were a helpless and vulnerable infant, but it is hard to believe about any adult.

Man evolved in primitive societies with very limited choice in mate selection. It is not clear that the wide range of choice we now have in relationships improves most people's relationship life that much. Those "gourmets of the single life" who chose variety and a succession of relationships, however, do have an appropriate arena for their life game in modern urban society.

Others are handicapped in starting a new

relationship by an apparently inflated opinion of their own worth. "I'm too good for..." Often this conceit hides a fear of being overwhelmed by others with clear wishes and viewpoints.

The unavailability of the kind of person you want is a complicated issue. True, there may be a shortage of women in Anchorage, Alaska. Even that difficulty doesn't seem insurmountable to me as I recall a woman who went to Anchorage in response to a letter from a former classmate. Lonely, he had written to Edna that jobs were plentiful, as were men. "...I always did like him," she remarked to me as she went off "job-hunting" in Anchorage.

Women are widely seen as disadvantaged as far as age is concerned, older men having more opportunities than older women. However, an important statistic to remember is that two-thirds as many women remarry in the 45-54 year old group as men. Certainly the handicap is not overwhelming and leaves a lot of room for individual effort.

Understanding Your Process

The first step in finding someone new is under-standing the method, the "process" you've used in the past. The emphasis of this book is awareness of your own "process", your own functioning, and its contribution to your life in all areas. While the world is very imperfect, some people do better with it than others. In order for you to get the most out of your life, you need to become aware of what you actually do to help make your life how it is. Understanding your process is theoretically very simple, and you are the best person to do it. You need however to become a neutral and careful observer of your thoughts and actions, how you become stimulated, what agitates you, and what your responses are. Often psychotherapy is necessary; many people find that they need the objective attitude of another person before they can learn to objectively observe themselves. To understand your own process you need to observe yourself uncritically, and trust that you can stand to know what you learn about yourself. After all, there is an old saying that "Every man has earned hanging at least once."

By process I mean the actual succession of events, internal and external, which accompany or precede any "activity" or topic. I am going to illustrate by using some disguised cases, how crucial is the understanding of your own process in choosing someone new. It is often easier to see how others create their own lives than to face the methods of our own madness. All of us have made friends in the past; how this occurs is crucial in understanding the form and course of our intimate relationships. Perhaps you will find yourself among these cases, or more likely, learn how to write down your process in a similar manner.

I don't quite recall how Tommy first came to see me, I do remember pleasant therapy hours, walking with him on the heavily shaded streets behind my office. A man who thought of himself still as a flower child while clearly a tall, wiry, and rugged male, he complained of not being able to find a girl friend. He had recently returned from a wandering journey through India and the Middle-East. He hadn't the money to take a girl out. Bright, he had a hard time starting at the bottom in straight society. He was convinced that he would stay for thirty years at close to the entry level job once he began. This had happened to his father.

"Flower Children," he said, "are no longer popular in the United States." Very shy, concerned about his height and thinness, he only mentioned two decent relationships. The first, in India, grew out of a friendship with a hippie couple. His male friend had felt the need to wander off for several months. Tommy remained a frequent visitor and companion to the "girl-friend" and soon she was his girl friend. Wanderers need a resting place and a return and after several months Tommy's friend returned. There were long and tearful scenes, but before very long Tommy was without a woman again.

His best experience was with a woman who had found him in the co-educational showers of the Jerusalem YMCA (so he said). A wanderer like him, she seemed to need a friend as she wandered from Israel to Spain. There she suddenly needed to return home, and bade Tommy a warm and fond farewell. "...She was so beautiful," Tommy said wistfully.

Unaggressive and unassuming, while tall and strong, Tommy was truly the ideal man to protect a beautiful American woman in the middle east. Too shy and ambivalent to make any substantial offer or effort on his own to win a woman, he frequently had to be satisfied with his friends' leavings.

In therapy he talked about finding a woman for himself. As his morale improved he began to circulate socially more. Once again, among his friends there was someone who needed to "go away" for a few months, and Tommy began to spend time with the "girl friend." Soon they were living together and Tommy could leave his van, where he had been living primarily. Sexually, he was in bliss, yet to me he confessed that he "didn't know about making a commitment . "...She's not exactly right... She wants to settle down and go to school, I don't know if that's what I want."

Bobby returned from from his wanderings and after a bit, Tommy was eased out. There was much pain for Tommy, and awkwardness for all. There were many conversations about the importance of friendship, and all swore undying loyalty on a friendship basis. Tommy was once again alone.

There are many ways to understand and respond to Tommy's history. Many people will respond initially in a critical and moralistic way. It is easy to feel superior to him.

From the standpoint of self knowledge, it is important to understand that Tommy had these critical and moralistic ideas too; these were what stood in the way of his truly knowing himself. Of course it was difficult for him to acknowledge his passivity, and to face his modus operandi as a "scavenger of women." It was much easier for him to talk about changes that he had not the will to make. It is easy to criticize his way of being in the world with women, and Tommy would be the first to join in the criticism. Actually, he harmed no-one.

Tommy himself felt discouraged by what he experienced as the fickleness of women. When one of his relationships would end, he was disheartened, without the energy to begin again for some time. From the perspective of an outsider it is easy to see how his modus operandi produced the kind of women who abandoned him. They never really chose him in the first place. He was a stand-in, too overwhelmed by his feelings of inadequacy to pursue a woman on his own.

No doubt a series of "acts of will," a totally new leaf in regards to women would help in this case. Such conversion experiences are wonderful when they occur. Self knowledge and self acceptance however offers another path. Thus, if Tommy had truly accepted his style of functioning he could have done several things. He might have had a series of affairs, until or unless he genuinely changed. Or, facing his limitations, he might have committed himself to one of the women who passed through his life, recognizing that his passive manner and difficulties in stuggling for what he preferred made his choices limited.

Ann presents a more typical problem. Ann attracted men easily. She experienced all men as mainly interested in sex. She felt betrayed and devalued as a person by what she saw as the primary male interest, and in response generally felt sexually cold and unfeeling. Her sexually unfeeling attitudes and responses didn't help her relationships last.

Despite her dislike of men's insistent sexuality, she dressed in a flirtatious and provocative way. The conflict between her behavior and attitudes in this area are fairly common, and are a good place to begin a discussion of the problem of "objectification."

Objectification

Our commercial society develops in us the habit of evaluating and dealing with people in terms very similar to the way we deal with cars and video recorders. While primitive people give human characteristics to trees, rocks, and natural forces, we give functional and limited characteristics to people. We speak only briefly to the shoemaker and know nothing about his private life. Our physicians are strangers in white coats who marry and divorce in secret and away from us. Similarly, women are often narrowly evaluated according to their sexual characteristics.

Few people want to be reduced to the status of a thing, even if it is a thing of beauty. There is a tendency in good relationships to go further to a more multi-faceted friendship that embodies all the many different parts of a person. When we sense that we are related to only in a single dimension, we often feel objectified and used. At the same time, it is clear that we invite our use. Ann for instance attracted men by her beauty, yet was annoyed that all she got was men who were interested primarily in her looks and the sexual allure she projected. Like many attractive women, she was afraid to give up leaning on her attractiveness. She finally faced the fact that the men she attracted were appropriately responding to her mode of dress. With a great deal of anxiety she entered a new world, changing her hair style and color. Braving her fear that no one would be interested in her other aspects, she went back to school and attracted a college professor.

Often people, hung up around problems of their

own objectification by others, talk of their need for love. Unfortunately, the love they want is love without any responsibility on their part to take the other's needs into consideration. Perhaps they are so disgusted with being an object, a delivery system for someone else's wishes that they can't face being responsible in any way. The unconditional love that they want, we only offer to our infants. From adults and older children we have expectations, sooner or later. The desire for unconditional love is very strong and very widespread and seems to be part of the longing that animates many love affairs. Presumably we didn't get enough of it as infants ourselves. When I sometimes hear women speak disparagingly about men wanting mothering, I think of the need for unconditional love, present too in women in different ways.

Some men and women seemingly embrace their objectification, their one dimensionality. Women who can comfortably use their sex appeal to start a relationship, men who lean heavily on their larger earning power, or their physical strength and can easily offer those aspects of themselves in a relationship, find beginning relationships easy. Their problems come later.

Often the woman who uses her objectification and "lets herself be used" finds it difficult to have a sexually gratifying life. Men who are focused on their provider role often can't let themselves relax with a woman. They see the relationship as depending so heavily on exchange values that they don't trust themselves in the relationship as a person could with a friend.

Both men and women who use their objectification,

their "market place value" to promote their relationships seem to complain a great deal about the
shallowness of their partners. More important is the
self-recognition that they are relying on a tactic that
brings them the kind of companions they have.
Recognition of this truth begins no easy solution. The
feared alternative is at least temporary loneliness.
Underneath neurotic symptoms and self deceiving
solutions are real dilemmas, which are painful to face.

Love Affairs With The Currently Married

The search for complete and fulfilling relationships
often involves dissatisfied and incompletely married
men and women. The novelist Adam Lelchuk describes
the frequent affairs of the modern american male as the
contemporary equivalent of hunting! An exciting and
(relatively) safe pastime in a too civilized society. Ted,
however, took his affairs, ostensibly at least, more
seriously. From a working class family, he was attracted
to proper and elegant women. A rather straightforward
lawyer, he prided himself on not lying. "I teach my
clients that it's not lying when you don't tell
everything," he liked to say.

In his affairs, Ted made no false promises, and
presented himself in his simple, blunt, and friendly way.
Not unattractive, he managed to have lovers, especially
when trying a long case out of his usual surroundings.
He could not understand why he always seemed to
connect with the "wrong women." It didn't take an
overwhelming amount of work with me for him to
discover how his process created his unsatisfactory

choices. For the women who were drawn to him were rule breakers and rebels. A petty criminal, now reformed and an answering service operator, was one. A social worker who had been a revolutionary, a drug dealer, and a saboteur in the sixties was another.

The elegant women he desired were also much more conventional in their values and while they might have an affair, it needed to be in the context of a "serious" relationship...moving towards marriage. Only a rule breaker who wasn't too concerned with social mores could sanction a relationship outside the norm of monogamy. For women concerned enough with conventional values to have mastered them weren't interested in a man who was almost a bigamist in his attitude. His honesty didn't help him in those relationships.

More married men (and women) have affairs than leave their spouse, so such choices have problems for those who want all the privileges and responsibilities of married life: joint residence, sexual exclusivity, shared economics, children, and social respectability. Of course, such affairs leave one with a great deal of free time! They are easy to end. If an established relationship is what you want, it will probably not happen out of your first affair with a married person. Yet...a patient of mine, happily married for the second time, liked to answer her girl friends' question," Where did you find him?". She would say, "Where all the good men are, with their wives."

It is very important that you face the reasons someone from the other sex wants you. Who you present yourself to be, and what you want from another person, must have some congruence. Authenticity, being yourself, showing your true feelings, being honest are important when building a close, intimate relationship. No close relationship can last when the other discovers you're not the person you pretended to be. Still, a problem arises when an inconsistent and divided person like Ted attempts honesty, which is not life's only value. Other people may not want their particular combinations of quirks and whims. An honest quasi bigamist has small place in polite society.

Limitations and Consequences

A highly energetic and beautiful woman got tired of her boy friends always "hitting on" her for sex. She was happy to find a man who seemed less sexually needy and possessively intrusive into her business relationships with men. After marriage, her relief turned to sadness, as she faced the fact that she had a good business partner, a kind husband, but a very minimal sexual partner.

Renee's process with men seemed more opaque. I was surprised to discover that this rather well bred and attractive businesswoman and mother of two would only "date" black men. Her relationships were a constant source of discouragement. Despite her willingness to ignore convention in this area, I soon discovered that she would never let one of her lovers stay with her for the entire night. Her racial preferences had their limit. A very determined, self-reliant person, she had walked out of her traditional marriage to a "male chauvinist." At the time she had no job or money and had her children to raise.

As I came to know her and her life situation more fully, I began to understand and respect her choices better. Intuitively she sensed that bringing a new husband into her life would make the raising of her children more difficult.

This realization reflects much clinical and scientific opinion. For while children may do better in a well integrated family, reestablishing one after divorce is often extremely difficult. Renee had had two white boyfriends after her marriage. One was a rather poor but warm and intelligent man with no earning power; the other a psychiatrist whom her children had cared about. He had a fine capacity for being a father and husband and had shown it in his first marriage. Now he seemed no longer interested in raising a second family, "...or he just didn't find me worth it," said Renee. Although Renee was voluptuous and more sexually adequate than most women, she was no longer young, and did not have a conventionally pretty face. I came to realize that she had assessed her chances at marriage and decided at some level that it was unlikely that she would find the sort of man she needed to help her father her children.

She gave up that goal and decided to capitalize on her virtues and desirability to black men. She no longer had marriage on her mind. She found boyfriends for herself, yet it was difficult for her to accept the limitations she herself had built into her relationships. Either her choices or her values had to change. For although she loved black men and came to feel quite sympathetic to their problems, she could never seriously consider marriage with one, and therefore felt protected.

One thing I have learned from my patients: each one seems to have developed a method of choosing, a way of operating in the heterosexual world. This way is sometimes easy in the beginning, and for people whose lives aren't working well in this area, difficult in the end. I believe that when relationships fail, part of the difficulty in starting fresh is the recognition that one's way of being in the world probably doesn't work well. Underneath the rationalization that there are no suitable partners is the recognition that perhaps one's own modus operandi must change. Still, sometimes we give up our "systems" too soon; for with persistence we may find someone with whom our system will work.

The easiest way to begin anew is to use the old methods that have worked in the past, and accept their limitations. Every form of life has some disappointments. Perhaps a small change in your system will mean a big change in whom you have as your companion. Ann, for instance, who disliked being seen primarily as a one dimensional sex object, chose to present herself somewhat one-dimensionally in another area, one that she liked better.

A good strategy, a good method doesn't work all the time. You may have chosen a method that will work in the long run, which means that you have to accept occasional failures, and be persistent. While honesty, for instance, is in many ways the best policy for intimate relationships, certainly there are times when it will make your friends mad. Safer policies work more often, but may not give you what you need. Examine yourself to see what is your acceptable failure rate. Do you need to be right, to win all the time? If so, you probably ought to stay at home, the world is too problematic. At the other end, if all your adventures fail, you're being foolish, unrealistic, reaching beyond your grasp.

Questions To Ask Yourself

Writing down the answers to these questions is a good way to learn to know your process more. Write them down, and then put the answers away for a few days and look at your answers again. If you wish, you can record your answers on a tape player and listen to them again.

1. How did you connect in your last two relationships? An answer like, "He just walked up and said hello" is not allowed. Where were you that he said hello? What did you do? What are you responsible for that made that happen?

2. What built-in disadvantages or negative consequences did your method of connecting with someone new have?

3. What is an acceptable risk level for you? Be realistic. If failure crushes you, follow a conservative policy. If boredom plagues you, more risk is in order.

3
Choosing the Right One

Understanding why we choose who we choose is crucial in improving our intimate life. One way to understand our intentions is to look at the similarities in the people we choose. Perhaps in this way we can better face our hidden intentions.

Every choice has consequences, problems it too entails. Thus, if you are attracted to beauty, expect the beautiful people you meet to know the worth their beauty commands, or to value and assess a like beauty in you, too. Understanding that, you may complain less of fickleness. You may have chosen what lawyers call an "attractive nuisance." Others call such a person a temptation.

One of the best ways to understand your choices is to understand your own way of meeting people. Understanding your process is central. Only through realizing how your activities create your life can you exert control over it. Thus, hanging out in a bar to find new people may be a quick way to meet someone new. It means also that you have no cause to complain about your sweetie's alcoholic habits. These are simple examples. Most of us can see these effects. We deceive ourselves crucially in more subtle ways. Making ourselves conscious of our motives, of our process is crucial to improving our choices and our life in general. The importance of self-awareness in matters of love is crucial. Often when someone complains or apologizes to me for having acted terribly, I'll say, "What a pity you didn't do it deliberately." My remark is surprising to them, until I explain further that whatever pleasure their misdeed offered them is diminished when they take no credit for it; neither, then, do they understand their power and choice. In my way, I am encouraging them to "own" their actions. In this way their "process" can become conscious, present. When you kid yourself about your motives, your behavior becomes opaque, at least to yourself. Our friends can often see us more clearly. In the mad chaos of the world there is little certainty, less probably in love than in all else but war. While we have limited power to control others, we have (we hope) somewhat more power to control ourselves. We can't control ourselves when we leave part of ourselves out of discussion: then those parts act in a hidden and covert fashion.

The influence that I have seen in out-of-awareness psychological processes was most dramatically shown to me in a small group exercise. I asked each group member to think of something about his current life that he didn't like that seemed like an affliction, a pain, a trouble. Then I asked each person to think of the first time in his life that he had "looked forward" to that event, or anticipated it. The next part of the exercise had each person think of an intermediate time point between the earliest "looking forward," and the present unfortunate state of affairs. In almost every case, the current state of affairs was expected, and in a way selected. Disease, bad marriages, divorce, lack of money were all expectations which then acted as "attracting visions of the future" in some way. The early fantasies we have of our adult life often act as some master blueprint. While we think of these ideas as fears, when they are in our head as future expectations they act like a master plan, and it is important that we get to know them.

It is important to remember that our "bad" choices may have been valuable, even growthful under the circumstances. Through knowing them, through owning them we can change them, or modify them. Ted's choice of rule breaking women meant he could have his affairs with little lying and false promises. Ann's choice of inaccessible men meant that she had time to study and felt she wasn't compelled to "take care" of a man.

To say that there are payoffs in your poor choices doesn't mean that you are deliberately choosing trouble for yourself, or sabotaging yourself. Frequently you have other motives. Failure is a natural byproduct of these motives, not a deliberate choice in itself. It's an old saw that a good mechanic often drives a car on the verge of a breakdown. He's not worried, he knows how to fix cars. Ann doesn't have to look for a busily occupied man. If a handsome man comes along whom many would choose if he were single, all she has to do is not reject him as her more discriminating sisters would. Then she hasn't really chosen a married man, she just hasn't rejected him.

In understanding your choices, identifying the true

choice point is often important. A friend of mine who loves good food and has little ability to resist temptation, rarely steps into a fine restaurant and turns down most dinner invitations. He knows the almost inevitable consequences that occur when he is around good food and doesn't delude himself about his process. Alcoholics Anonymous teaches that the beginning of change is recognizing your addiction and calling yourself an alcoholic. From the standpoint of awareness, strength may consist of acknowledging, of "owning" your weaknesses.

Tommy didn't see himself as choosing to involve himself with his friend's girl friend, but he hung around no other women, developed no other relationships, and was sexually starved. To an outsider, the consequences were expected. While we are always free to choose, some choices are much more difficult than others. It is like taking one fork of the road: changing your mind may mean a tedious return or a long walk along rough country.

Facing a similar problem led a somewhat controversial obstetrician, working amongst the poor people of the Appalachian hills, to give up his ineffective birth control lectures to his patients who continued having more children then they could care for or afford. As the mothers would face the delivery of their fourth or fifth child they would complain bitterly about how little they needed another child to care for, another mouth to feed. They denied any need for birth control at that point, for they swore they would never even have sex again! These mothers wouldn't own their sexual neediness. Of course they didn't need to make birth control plans. In a few months he would see them again expecting another child.

Not acknowledging their sexual desire meant they couldn't plan for it. Instead, they were "overcome" by their feelings. As a result, he began to pressure his patients to allow him to perform sterilizations as part of the delivery procedure.

So ask yourself this about your bad choices, no matter how awful they seem. How did I benefit from this? What good (no matter how small or obscure) came of it all? Am I really free of the need that I gratified with my "poor" choice? Perhaps I ought to incorporate that need into my conscious self, like an Appalachian mother.

Impact of Early Learning

Perhaps this is a place to look at our parents, and their impact on our love choices. At times I think that our minds have a special relational sphere that looks like Swiss cheese. The holes we have in our heads are relational holes, made mostly by our earliest and most important relationships. When someone new comes along, we try and fit them into an empty hole. If they happen not to fit at first, we work a bit to make them fit our model. For this is what we know, this is what we have habitual ways to deal with. With this model in mind, ask yourself, What about Mommy or Daddy or sister Jane am I looking for in my new intimate relationships? What expectations did they leave me with, about close relationships?

Sarah came to me early in my career and stayed a long time. When I first began to work with her I gave her a general personality questionnaire, one that provided an approximate measure of many different psychological traits. Surprisingly, she scored somewhat hostile and suspicious. I found this hard to believe, never having known her in her relationship with me to be anything but friendly and helpful. Over time, as I watched her dating behavior, and understood her relationship to her father, those old test results made more sense to me.

Daddy was a violent and unpredictable alcoholic. He was also the parent who had loved her dearly when she was very small. Sarah had a particularly painful memory of waking up in the middle of the night and going to get a glass of water. Her father came roaring at her from nowhere and chased her in terror back to bed. His drinking was somewhat hidden, so his behavior was all the more shocking and unexplainable to her. In her family environment he was quite overwhelming in general and Sarah developed a tough argumentative side to help cope with her familial environment. Pretty, she didn't have a great deal of trouble beginning relationships, but she often seemed excessively afraid of vigorous "tough" guys. She gravitated to quite less frightening and less threatening men. These relationships collapsed whenever in a fight she let loose her rage. This tactic, one she learned to help her cope with her father, drove her boyfriends away. Those who were more robust in this area, strong fighters in their own right, reminded her of him and frightened her.

Understanding her process meant for Sarah realizing her fear of certain kinds of men. This fear drove her to less threatening men, to whom she herself was somewhat intimidating.

Therapists are accustomed to hearing patients blame parents and we hear many tales of bad and inadequate parents. Joe's mother has my first prize. At least three men killed themselves because of her. Even when she was over sixty years old, she could lure some old codger into hanky-panky at a wedding reception. While Joe's father was in the army during the Korean War, Joe was badly beaten by his mother on occasion. Imagine Joe's later reaction to a seductive woman, or to an angry woman. Of course they reminded him of his hated and seductive mother. (She was a bit flirtatious with him too, routinely calling him in as an adolescent to help her with her brassiere or girdle.) Both Sarah and Joe have had great difficulty coping with their opposite sex parent's legacy. In each case the parent offered the promise of real love as well as great danger and destructiveness. Thus, both of them have had great difficulty finding someone appropriate to commit to, without that person also being terribly frightening.

Extreme cases are easy to understand. Less painful histories present more subtle issues in adult character. Pamela's parents were always "working" on their relationship. Pamela's mother was more determined to make her marriage work well. "I'm not going to give up," she would declare as she would troop herself and her kids from one therapist to another. Her husband, a rather tyrannical minister, wouldn't bother to come. He had a poor opinion of psychology, although he didn't quite see it as the work of the devil. He had little use for therapists and most therapists had a poor opinion of him as a husband or father. He was dictatorial and controlling and Pamela's parents had a rather poor marriage by most criteria. Pamela's father was terribly overbearing and Pamela's mother retreated into apparent stupidity and other forms of hidden resentment.

Pamela of course had no desire to repeat her mother's life. She tried to liberate herself from her conditioning by seeking out men as unlike her father as possible. Yet she was never quite happy with the wimpy and uncommitted men she ended up with. Of course she was suspicious of marriage in general. Her parents had what they said was a "good" marriage and she knew how awful that was.

Pamela's story illustrates several points. Certainly the effects of her parents' miserable marriage weren't as paralyzing as, say, a painful divorce and separation. Pamela avoided repeating her mother's mistakes with the help of her aversion to strong men, which certainly included all dominant men like her father, as well as many others. While her aversion protected her, it also left her somewhat unsatisfied. As she grew to understand the basis of her aversion, she was able to modify her choices somewhat. More aware, she was able to avoid her father's replica without choosing flaky men.

Questions To Ask Yourself

Writing down the answers to these questions is a good way to learn to know your process more. Write them down, and then put the answers away for a few days and look at your answers again. If you wish, you can record your answers on a tape player and listen to them again.

1. What is similar in the people I choose, physically, socially, economically, sexually? Who was a person from the past that I remember first having these character-istics?

2. What do I get in return for my "bad" choices? Can I see any positive advantages to these choices? What do these choices protect me from?

3. How do I not own my sexual neediness?

4
Sex

Sex is certainly central to getting connected in a heterosexual relationship. There has been a great deal of debate as to when to begin the explicitly sexual part of a relationship. Before birth control marriage seemed a prior necessity to many. A current commentator on social rules and etiquette states "Dating consists of eating, conversation and sexual intimacy. In the beginning the emphasis is on the first activity, and shifts slowly through the second to the last."

Beginning a relationship sexually often creates a quick intimacy that may dissolve as quickly, or may last, despite the fears of traditional women. Putting a lot of energy into a relationship at the beginning can be an important way to demonstrate seriousness and caring. Whether or not one has sex at the beginning seems less important than the context in which it occurs, as far as the implications for the future are concerned. If, for instance, a rather sexually experienced person says that they are passionately interested in a new friend, but doesn't want to have sex with them, a somewhat contradictory message is sent. The best policy here as in so many places is talk about it. Talk about the context for

43

your beginning, what you are trying to begin, if beginning something is what you are up to.

The male culture supports its members beginning sexually. Then each man proceeds to have as much of a relationship as he desires or can maintain. The female culture supports its members having a relationship first, and then having as much sex as seems suitable to the woman and the relationship. This is strikingly apparent in the homosexual world. There, male homosexuals are comparatively heavily into frequent and anonymous sex; female homosexuals are heavily focused on relationships. (Of course there are numerous individual and group exceptions to this statistically based picture.) What happens between a man and a woman in this area is really a struggle over the rules of the game: shall the game begin on men's rules or women's rules. Of course there are individual differences: some women are more interested in sex than some men, at any given point in their lives.

This perspective makes it easier to deal with the issue of when to begin sex. When your new friend doesn't want to start your way, that doesn't necessarily mean a lack of love, caring, or sexual interest. Probably it is a skirmish over power. The senior United States negotiator in the Middle East, Phillip Habib, apparently earned great distinction in a previous negotiation. He spent months negotiating with the North Vietnamese on the shape of the negotiating table! Such preliminary discussions often determine the shape of what follows.

Like all social rules or "norms", custom lags behind technology and practice. Easy birth control, anti-biotic remedies for venereal disease, labor-saving devices that made women's energy less crucially necessary to run a house, all these new factors have changed the context for sexual relationships. We don't yet know what works, and for whom under these changed circumstances. The Herpes plague and dreaded AIDS have once again introduced a new factor. In a time of change in sexual relationships like ours, the ability to constantly communicate, hear the other person, as well as your own stirrings, is absolutely necessary to adaptation. Anything less is like trying to sail a ship through a storm with a frozen rudder.

The Importance of Meaning

More than most areas of man's activity, sex is hard to separate from all of one's feelings. Thus I was surprised one day when a patient of mine called up because of an emergency. He was unable to "make it" with a woman. He was concerned with what was wrong with him.

"What was she like, Jack?" I asked him.

"Nothing special," he replied. "Not bad looking."

"Had you known her long?" I asked.

"I just met her," he replied.

"Did you like her?" I finally asked. "Not particularly.. .but I didn't dislike her," was his answer.

Somehow he expected to have good sex with someone who he hardly knew and didn't excite him.

Women make similar mistakes. Thus a woman announced to a patient of mine that he wasn't loving her properly. He was somewhat more psychologically knowledgeable. They had being making love quite happily up until that point. "Your pleasure is your business," he announced. "If you want orgasms with me, I'm sure you can have them. I think you're mad at me." She acknowledged her resentment, and after a short chat, they had excellent sex. While its probably true that women, on the average, prefer more time spent in foreplay than men, often their attitude is caused by the symbolic meaning of the time and effort spent.

Another way that we can understand the psychological aspect of sex is through our understanding of being ticklish. When we are stroked or touched by someone with whom we don't want sex, we often are ticklish. Part of this response has to do with the nature of the touch contact, another part has to do with the appropriateness of the person for a sexual contact, as well as our mood of the moment. In the laughter and spontaneous movements of our response to being tickled there is a partial energy discharge. It is a less complete discharge than in good sex, but also gratifying.

Erica Jong in her book "Fear of Flying" describe the "zipless fuck", by which she means sex without a meaningful relationship. That too is psychological. To be excited by someone's good looks or their purely sexual approach is not a purely physical response, it is a response to an idea about desire. It is easy to see why the somewhat auto-biographical heroine would be excited by the idea of a "zipless fuck." Stuck in a loveless marriage, sex with a basically unknown stranger would allow her to leave her life structure basically unchanged. Many married people actually choose such liaisons when their marriage is without sex and they are afraid of divorce.

Fantasies of sex with a mysterious stranger, even extending to rape, are not uncommon in young women in traditional societies. In these societies, outside of marriage any sex is inappropriate. Marriage is often long delayed. Sex with any member of their social group seems inappropriate. It is not some strange lust that drives them to these fantasies but the lack of any other socially adequate solution.

What a person is looking for sexually-socially can sometimes be understood through dreams and masturbatory fantasies. Thus it was with the distinguished gentleman who came to see me early in my career. In his sixties, he complained of a poor relationship with his wife. He seemed to be without any significant sexual interest in her, which might have been part of the reason she gave him a difficult time. As in many psychological issues, causes bring effects which strengthen causes.

His wife seemed to be a strong woman who wanted things to be done her way. He was quite handsome looking, striding along with a cane. He had spent a number of years out of the country on business. No wonder she learned how to run her household, one that he now had to struggle to fit into. After a time in therapy he revealed something of his time abroad. He had lived for some time in a brothel while in southeast Asia. "...Quite innocently," he assured me. His dreams also had an Asian flavor.

In his dreams he was surrounded by naked women who would bow to him and offer various good things. At times he would beat them in his dreams. At last I understood his cane, unusual in a healthy man, even of his age. I also understood that his domineering wife had no chance with him sexually. That certainly wasn't what he wanted.

It is important to understand these excluded parts of oneself. Dreams, which often include at night what we exclude by day, are a way to understand what we may have felt more comfortable ignoring. Sex is also a way to connect with parts of yourself that you have ignored or repressed. Thus dirt and "sordid" sex can appeal to an exclusively correct and clean person. I have seen strong dominating professional women take as a lover men who are brutalizing. In ordinary life they have cut themselves off from their caring and feminine side. Only submitting in the privacy of this intimate relationship allows them to recover some feeling of "femininity." The opposite pole of this problem is expressed by the burly truck-driver who finds feminine underpants worn in secret a way to get in touch with his own neglected softness.

Physical Aspects of Sexual Activity

Sex certainly has a physical as well as a psychological aspect. A very important physical factor that affects sexual life is the "armoring" that occurs in the body when we habitually control our feelings. Feelings are expressed with the aid of special muscle groups, and when you hold your feelings back on a general basis, these muscles become very tense. Being uptight has a literal meaning... Relaxation of these muscles is important to allow for the natural flow of feeling, so important in sexual activity. This is why massage often helps improve your sexual life. Dance will also loosen up the body and allow for the flow of feelings; which is how it often frees up people for sexual activity .

One special physical characteristic of sexual activity that makes it different from other emotional activity is that the two main emotional expressive systems have to come into action in turn. When you are unduly goal oriented and have fixed ideas as to what feelings you should express, or are trying to not express your fear or anger, it is hard to have much of a sexual response. Your body is busily dealing with the held back fear or anger. Some of the emotional system that is used for sexual activity is occupied with holding back another set of feelings, and is not free to respond sexually. In order to have a new set of feelings, the first set of feelings has to "run its course."

Many people believe that they should generally control their feelings. They don't cry easily or often. Their anger is expressed in muted ways, as is their joy. No surprise that their sex life is also flat and muted.

Similarily, it is extremely important to take general care of your body. Sex is an activity that requires a degree of physical fitness, especially for men. Don't expect your body to function sexually if it doesn't function much physically or emotionally in any other area of your life.

One important way you may have learned to control your feelings is through holding your breath. (When I ask the audience in public meetings, "How many have learned this?" from one-quarter to one-half say "Yes.") Once learned, this method tends to operate automatically in many emotional areas. Feared feelings are controlled by reducing the amount of oxygen flowing into the body.

After once encouraging an isolated young woman to become aware of when she held her breath, she returned to her next therapy hour, angrily complaining. "...I don't see why you told me to be aware of when I hold my breath. I did it the other evening while watching television alone. So I let myself breathe, and all that happened is that I ended up realizing how lonely I felt and crying by myself."

One of the easiest ways to improve your sexual life is to focus on your breathing during sexual activity. If you notice that you are holding your breath, experiment with breathing more fully and see what happens to your excitement level.

Orgasms release muscular tension in a similar way to fits of intense crying, or outbursts of rage. Which method we prefer to use to discharge our tension is a function of many factors. Often sexual feelings, which involve great intimacy, are difficult to share in a relationship where there has been much criticism and destructive hostility. In these relationships couples find it safer and easier to discharge their emotional energy through fighting. This is part of the reason why it is sometimes easier to begin a new sexual relationship, than to improve an old one. Rage and tears require less vulnerability than sexuality for many people.

I often find myself listening in an annoyed fashion to the following complaint: "...My (husband, boy friend, lover) doesn't want sex." Usually what the woman speaking to me means is that her man is not romantically, aggressively, or even actively pursuing sex with her. This lack of expressed sexual interest is often hurtful, but it certainly isn't the same as not wanting sex. Many men also like to feel an active sexual interest from their women: it is a great turn-on. The struggle here is over energy, ego, interest, as much as it is over sex itself.

It is important to recognize that the permeation of sex with non-physical desires expresses itself in the physical. I see few true hedonists. Few people are really into physical pleasure in other areas than sex. When they want something special in sex, it is for psychological reasons. Usually I observe issues like bargaining, specialness and proof of devotion. Who is going to give more energy to sex by making the initial overtures is really important. Of course it is important in a dozen other areas too. Who sits down first at the dinner table and waits while the other finishes up some last minute activity is a similar issue. Similar too is the issue of who is first to say a fight has gone too long, or too far, or was really a mistake. Parallel to a women's desire to be courted as a proof of devotion seems to be the man's desire for the woman's complete sexual surrender. No orifice barred, no possible sexual activity denied. Then he will know he is really loved.

The complaint, "He wants oral sex with me but he's not willing to do the same" is a complaint about who does more for whom in the relationship, played out in the sexual arena. I often see the statement "I need clitoral stimulation," as having that meaning.

Universally, the men I have worked with are unable to have sex unless there is something about the whole situation that is mentally exciting: conquest, closeness, security, comfort, anonymity, communion, aggression, hostility towards another person not present, communion with nature—there is always an idea present and necessary for a man to have an erection. I hope this knowledge does something for all those women who feel physically used by men. For a woman, this also is largely true, although differences in physiology allow a woman to participate in sex more passively and to a degree, without interest and pleasure.

Sex is not an isolated function. My observation of the majority of sexual difficulties is that they can be resolved in one of three ways: 1. Improving or resolving problems in the relationship; 2. The more sexually desirous partner needs to non-defensively pursue sex more aggressively; and 3. The body needs to be loosened and improved to enable it to support sexual release. Many of us will not be harmed if we work on all three areas.

Questions To Ask Yourself

Writing down the answers to these questions is a good way to learn to know your process more. Write them down, and then put the answers away for a few days and look at your answers again. If you wish, you can record your answers on a tape player and listen to them again.

1. What do you wish for sexually that you don't have? What is the meaning of this wish? What is missing in your ordinary life that you can get out of this sexual activity? Is sex the best avenue to fulfill that need?

2. How free are you in expressing your feelings in non sexual areas?

3. How tense and rigid is your body? What is your preferred method to loosen up?

5
Intensity and Diversity

A central issue for two people is deciding how much time they wish to be with each other. What each of us needs in terms of kind of time, kind of contact, and type of intimacy may be very different.

One problem that frequently comes up in this regard is the need that many people have to know that they are connected; this is frequently different from actually wanting to spend time with the other. When this happens, good-byes may be more intense and passionate than hellos. For couples in this place in their relationship the security of knowing that they have each other is more central than the actual pleasure in intimate contact. This kind of security is something we may have looked for from our mother. Playing, little children often run into the house to see if Mother is still there, only to run out into the world to play once more.

In Los Angeles I've noticed that established relationships between single adults can be better understood with the help of a "rule of thumb": One meeting or "date" a week means the relationship is declining or beginning. Two meetings a week is a steady state relationship, a relationship that might continue the way it is indefinitely. Three or four meetings a week characterizes a relationship that is building for a more involved and committed connection.

After I noticed this pattern in single adults, I found it interesting to read that the average sexual frequency for married adults is between two and three times a week! This seems more than coincidental, and underlines the importance of sex.

Neediness is Important

There is no relationship without neediness! Currently it is fashionable to downplay need in a relationship. Yet without a strong underlying need for another who will bother creating a relationship? I want to emphasize this point: there is no relationship without neediness.

"He is too needy," says one. "She wants too much," says another. "I don't need you, but I want you," says a more sophisticated person. These are the fashionable attitudes of the last decade.

This attitude was popularized in the "Gestalt Prayer" of Fritz Perls:

> "I didn't come into the world to live up to your expectations
> You didn't come into the world to live up to my expectations
> If perchance we meet, that's wonderful.
> If not, it can't be helped."

Fritz, who was at the forefront of the personal and social revolution of the sixties and seventies, was probably fairly unsuccessful in his relationships. He stayed unhappily married and separated from his wife until his death, although he enjoyed his life outside his marriage. He spent his last years apart from his wife with whatever other women he could find to enjoy. Out of his own misery he developed a preference for relationships that had a minimum of attachment. He had been, I believe, discouraged by his own experience and preferred relationships more like shipboard romances - without strings or future. A reading of his biography "Fritz" by Martin Shephard will confirm this.

While Fritz Perls came to his position out of his own pain, he became fashionable because his ideas fitted the sixties. Before that, he had gone into semi-retirement in Miami and had a minimal life despite writing a well received book. Many people were in like situations: they had married out of convenience and affection and they found their relationships stifling and destructive. Economically free, they regretted their lives "wasted" in unfulfilling relationships. The divorce rate zoomed.

Easier divorce hasn't solved the problem of marriage, although remarriage is easier than before. Marriages are only a little bit better than the people who make them, and their capacity to relate. What has changed about marriage is the strong social and economic necessity to remain in bad relationships, or in relationships that have outlived their reason for creation. With each member of a couple capable of economic self-support, the social stigma of divorce less severe, and the knowledge that the world is full or single or recently divorced people, the incentive to stay in a difficult marriage is often slight.

Much of the lack of fulfillment in contemporary

marriages could be handled by more frequent and clear declarations of need. Human beings are not computers and have a special capacity to respond to heartfelt and intimate requests.

Josie had come to see me for help in her second marriage. Her husband was busy working a long commute away from their condominium. She herself worked and took care of a child by her first marriage. She had been in therapy for her depression, but now she wanted help from me specifically for her marriage. Her husband joined her sporadically for sessions. He was very busy "building an economic future for us." Josie wanted to fix up the third bedroom of their house as a an artist's studio and she felt that all of the work would cost them about $1500. She was unhappy in the marriage and felt she wasn't getting what she needed: the main need she could specify was the studio. She hadn't asked Bill for the money to alter the room, or told him how important it was to her. I strongly encouraged her to do so.

One day she came in, full of news. "I did it," she said, "I finally did it."

"Did what," I asked.

"I told him," she said.

"Great," I said, "you finally told him you needed that studio. I'm glad to hear it."

"Oh no," she said. "I asked him for a divorce." She had found that easier than exposing her neediness and being vulnerable to her husband's possible "no." One thing we do need in a relationship is a neediness match. Often we see a hermit and a gregarious person together in a marriage. My fantasy is that they created each other. In the beginning their needs were only slightly different. In time, their demands on each other for more or less than the other wanted exaggerated their differences. Each recoiled from the other's model. Polarization was the result.

A neediness match is important sexually. A patient of mine ended her marriage of many years because her husband wanted sex three times daily. He managed to come home for lunch every day of the week! Such differences in sexual needs create tension in the relationship. There are many people who find occasional sex sufficient for them. Reconciling differences in needs are a central issue whether the need is for affection, attention or money. I have observed a great deal of self-deception in this area. Autonomy is a central value in our culture, and many people have a difficult time verbally acknowledging their need for other people. It is also difficult to admit that one's willingness to fill other's needs is limited. It is much easier to move away from this area and speak of "wanting" and not "needing."

Yet, sexual needs and contact needs are often a mask for reassurance. Do you really like skin contact, or are you asking for a proof of devotion. When you can distinguish between wanting love and affection, and needing to be reassured that your lover still cares, your relationships will do much better. A telephone call will handle reassurance and take much less time than a meeting! Perhaps more reassuring than love making is a solid talk about your mutual commitment to continue your relationship and stand by each other.

Passions Rise and Fall

When a love relationship begins "right" there is often a period of great passion and intimacy. We often dream and hope of this honeymoon. Some of the great lovers of the past have reported such interludes in their life. Errol Flynn, the great movie actor seems to have had his most ecstatic time as a young man with a Native Australian Bush Indian girl of about sixteen. They spent a summer together, but the world beckoned to Flynn and he left her. With the countless women who passed through his life afterwards he never seemed to have been quite as fulfilled.

Casanova reports a similar choice to give up a young woman early in his life. The story of how the happiest affair of this most infamous of lovers developed and ended is worth re-telling. He describes first meeting Julie when she was traveling with an officer, an Italian Captain. She herself was disguised as a junior officer. Soon she and Casanova ran off together. They were quite happy in Rome. She was about sixteen, a runaway, we would call her today. Then her family located her. It developed that she was from a powerful and noble house. Her protectors were courteous to Casanova and didn't rush him away. He was allowed to accompany Julie back towards her home in France. In Switzerland half-way back, they parted, etching their initials on a window in their inn.

Twenty years later Casanova finds himself in the same inn, staring at his initials and wondering how they had gotten there. Finally he recovered his memory of that early, passionate romance.

Not the end of the story. Even later he reports traveling in Spain, and taking refuge in a castle during a storm. The noble lord was away. Given shelter by the Castle's lady, he was received by her from behind a screen. It soon developed that it was Julie, fat, not wanting to let him see her as she then was; and he only spoke with her.

Somehow these great lovers of the past seem never to have recaptured that early joy, a rapture which seemed too casual and unimportant to hold. I think, as I write this, that perhaps that explains their compulsive love making later. Nothing compared with that early love they abandoned. Their report is similar to descriptions of the initiation of addictions: the first drink, the first gambling win, etc.

It is clear that most long relationships don't experience the constant sexual passion they may have had in the beginning. Some people are clearly not willing to settle for less excitement than the intense and intermittent passion of new beginnings. Perhaps these "love addicts" are more able to partially neutralize or cope with the pain of endings that leaves others unwilling to play love's game constantly. In this they are like other addicts: gamblers who love the excitement when the roulette wheel turns, with the possibility of a fantastic win. Loss seems far away; its consideration a distraction.

While the loss of sexual passion in a relationship is common, it certainly is not universal, and repays attempts at understanding. It seems common among other mammals. Laboratory experiments have shown that many male animals become sexually uninterested in their partner over time. These same animals become sexually excited and functional when a new female is introduced into their habitation. While the phenomenon seems continuous between human and animal species, human sexuality seems so much more mentally and psychologically effected that we need to look for psychological aspects. An accumulation of negative or slightly disappointing experiences with an old partner certainly plays a part. Many enter a sexual union with very high hopes; and when these are not gratified there is always the hope that another partner will have the "right stuff."

Jane, close to despair about the sexual emptiness of her second marriage of five years duration, recalled the beginning of her current relationship with her husband: "I met him with flowers, I was so excited to see him again, and I told him we in California celebrated our reunions in a jacuzzi. We both got terribly excited and then he told me he wouldn't make love until his divorce was final. I was stunned. I knew that he was religious and that his marriage had left him with tremendous feelings of sexual inadequacy. 'What does that matter', I thought. We wanted to make love so badly that we both hurt. We managed through the end of his divorce. My first husband had been so terrible sexually after that first horrid beginning on my honeymoon. I knew nothing. He would barely make love to me; half sleepy he would climb on me and in five minutes it would be over for him, with no caring for my needs and feelings. How could this man who I loved so much be any worse than that? Soon we were blissful...Sometimes we couldn't wait to get to the bedroom. We would tear each other's clothes off at the door to the apartment, and make love on the floor."

Yet, for this couple, passion wasn't enough to satisfy them. The world called: duties, interesting jobs, the possibility of fame seemed more important than constantly lying in each other's arms. What was once a loving embrace became a time-consuming pastime. Each expected the other to help them with their own separate different careers, while resenting the time they had to give up for the other's needs.

The call of the world takes many of us out of the love-nest as it took us out of our parents' home. Facing our need to be in the world, and reconstructing our relationship to give the world room within it, is important in a lasting relationship. When the world calls, the honeymoon frequently ends.

Reconciling different needs for intensity and diversity are central to creating and maintaining a relationship. Often we avoid facing our genuine differences in these areas by claiming we are not "loved" enough by our partner. Their caring may not be at the intensity we wish, or as time consuming for them.

A patient of mine got a scholarship to Oxford and just before he was about to leave, a classmate of his began an affair with him. Joyful, he was also perplexed. He had the world, now a woman had entered his life, how was he to choose?

"A loving woman is worth a year at Oxford any time," I said to him. He wasn't crazy about my suggestion. Suddenly Jack became creative and invited Roxanne to come with him. Still married, she didn't wish to leave her husband suddenly. My patient got patient instead of feeling hurt, critical, and not loved enough. He put off his trip, managed to delay his scholarship, and she eventually went with him. From the start their relationship has allowed them their needs outside their relationship with each other.

Not all of us can get it all, the intensity of a love relationship, and the new sights and sounds of a beckoning world. Central is the need to see that process as one always needing to be faced, even in the most glorious love affairs.

Questions To Ask Yourself

Writing down the answers to these questions is a good way to learn to know your process more. Write them down, and then put the answers away for a few days and look at your answers again. If you wish, you can record your answers on a tape player and listen to them again.

1. How much closeness do you want to another person and how much do you want to be in the world? Ask your friends if they agree.

2. Are you willing to be open about your neediness, or is this an embarassing topic for you?

6
Futurity—Long or Short

Our relationships are tremendously influenced by our expectations of their length. There are actually four actors in this drama: our expectations, our partner's expectations, our fantasies of his expectations, and his fantasies of our expectations. Many people find it difficult to disclose clearly and openly in this area. In this, as in many topics, know who you are. Only if you come to some clarity yourself, will you be able to communicate a position that your partner can choose to accept or reject.

Facing the subtle and conflicting aspects of your hopes and fears for security and adventure is not easy. While it is possible to change the nature of some relationships so they are more sedentary at one point, open at another, the options are not infinite. A relationship is partially created in a context. Change the context and the relationship changes. When I was a young adult in California it was a commonplace that a marriage made in another state would have a hard time surviving Southern California and its increased freedom and informality.

I distinguish four different expectations about time in a relationship:

1. A "brief encounter" or a "meeting with no tomorrow," as the French describe it.

2. An "ongoing" relationship: a steady state relationship; one with no explicitly stated goal, and an implicit understanding that it will continue as long as it suits both parties.

3. A relationship that is expected to end, either because the outside situation will change, or because it is clearly a temporary expedient.

4. A relationship that is expected to last indefinitely, although it is understood that it can end under certain circumstances.

Changing Expectations

Relationships work best when these expectations are known and shared. Many relationships work well inside one set of expectations about the future, but cannot survive a change, which turned out to be what happened to Fred.

A handsome and active man in his fifties, he had been keeping more or less steady company with a woman he liked and respected enormously. For some years she had wanted to move their relationship to be more "committed." She wanted them to live together. Because of the change that meant in the organization of their life style, it implied a very significant increase in the time they would be together. Their values were somewhat different, but they had enjoyed each other's company immensely.

They had struggled over this issue in the past. At times this struggle over changing the basis of their relationship led to their breaking off with each other for a time. Neither would find anyone whose company they preferred. As they got older each recognized that they had to do something about their future relational life. Shifting futurity, meant both real and symbolic changes. They were both strong independent people who liked to arrange their lives in a way that suited them. Symbolically, they had to face the meaning of a change in futurity. Any arrangements they made with each other were relatively permanent.

Fred, a builder and outdoorsman, was also something of a workaholic. Ida, a professional woman, enjoyed fine dinners, walking through fancy shopping districts, and travel involving staying at good hotels. These value differences created problems at vacation time; otherwise they were happy with each other.

Talking to me after their last attempt at shifting futurity had failed, Fred said, "...When we really tried to get together these last two weekends it was horrible. I guess all kinds of things were OK on a temporary basis, but when I think of living with Ida like this for the rest of my life, I don't like it."

Man does not live in the present alone, or even principally. Many psychologists presume that this is one of man's chief differences from animals, an advantage and a burden. Science Fiction heroes and Buddhist saints share with Errol Flynn an ability to (reputedly) live in the present. "Lose your mind and come to your senses," calls out a psychologist. Few of us can answer the call. We are oppressed by our imagining of future happenings . We wake up to a good day, the air is fresh as we drive in an open car to work. The breeze blows, the trees are green, our car handles well, and we begin to worry about what will happen at work, what our boss will say, the disasters that can happen. The beautiful day is forgotten. We live in our minds: future and past. Philosophers, poets, psychologists, all kinds of wise men have argued that this aspect of man makes us unhappy. "Be here now!" says one current teacher. "...and if not now, when?" said a Rabbi 2000 years ago, explaining Judaism in one breath.

Possibly we were one with nature as children. Some blame our child rearing methods, or our traumatic and unduly harsh birth for the loss of the ability to live animal-like, fully in the now. Perhaps true, but more certainly, that is only a partial truth. Our ability and disability to live in our heads is part of our mental equipment. Our ability and interest in planning, theorizing, making up explanations and acting on them as if they were real is part of what it means to be human. To know the nature of reality and to have foresight is our replacement for the instinctual senses of danger and direction.

Face it, a large part of our relationships thus is not what is in our relationships, but what we hope and imagine for the future. Even when we can't or won't put these expectations into words, they are part of the context, the background of our experience. Shifting futurity, shifting our expectations of the relationship is a major operation. We need to give much energy and attention to this change, as much perhaps as moving our relationship to a foreign country would require.

While shifting futurity is responsible for the end of some relationships, it is also the creator of others. Many have observed two old friends who suddenly discover the possibilities of their relationship when they are "ready to settle down."

In a "meeting with no tomorrow" there is no futurity, and often a great deal of spontaneity. A book on relationships is not a place to celebrate the joys and disasters of this kind of non-relationship. Occasionally such adventures are so mutually agreeable, that both parties decide to hold on to each other, and establish a continuing relationship with a different sense of futurity. The pleasures of brief relationships offer an acceptable life for many people; although they are reluctant to acknowledge this unfashionable choice. For most people, the pain of frequent endings outweighs the pleasures of beginnings.

The weakest form of real futurity is in an "ongoing" relationship. Implied in an "ongoing" relationship is that it will continue, unless something happens to change it. Traditionally, living together had this kind of futurity. The whole idea of living together that grew up in the the late nineteenth and early twentieth century was a reaction to the loveless marriages of those days. Many free-thinkers believed that relationships between men and women should not be encumbered by property, obligation and social pressure. A free relationship, it was thought and hoped, would be better since it would be based on current affection. Love would be better without matrimonial bonds to breed resentment and leave people together in the same household who would rather be somewhere else, with someone else. "Living together" can have that meaning today. Often however, it is seen as a step towards marriage. In this vein a man once asked me what I thought of living together before marriage. He had been having an affair while married for a number of years. Now he was considering divorcing his wife and marrying his lover, Renee.

I thought for a bit before replying, "By the time you've decided to live together, you've really decided that you want to marry her, and it's just a question of can you make a go of it. You might do better by marrying her. Few people like 'being on probation.' I've seen a relationship destroyed by a woman who was furious about that. Committing yourself to a longer future together by marriage shows more confidence, and most people respond well to that kind of energy, and the trust they sense."

Renee, whom he married after divorcing his wife and after living with her, lived out of town at that time. He had enjoyed a relationship that gave him a great deal of freedom and periodic intimacy. Perhaps that explains his reply: "...and what do you think about living together after marriage?"

For most of us marriage means living together after marriage, perhaps for the rest of our lives. Once living together is experienced as a part of a marriage it is more an engagement than a free relationship. For that reason, the term "fiance" is often used to describe the person one is living with. Until fairly recently one could sue for "breach of promise", a sure indication that expectations of futurity are involved. The breaking of an engagement required cause, fault was implied.

What is a Committed Relationship

Although the word "committed" is used often to describe relationships, it's meaning is unclear, or different to different people. The dictionary definition most close is "...to obligate or bind to a particular course of action or belief." It also means "... To punish or confine." A confusion between these meanings may be part of what makes the unexplained use of this term a cause of problems. The most frequent confusion has to do with the shifting nature of marriage bonds. In many primitive cultures, including the Jews of the Old Testament, marriage was simply public and open sexual cohabitation.

Today this can be done by "living together" or by marriage, one having full legal sanction, the other having a public sense in terms of friends and family, but not the larger legal system. Some people use the term "committed" to mean a relationship with a longer futurity. Others use it to mean everything personal, intimate, and long lasting that a marriage can be, without taking a position on the (immediate) necessity of that particular public form. Adding to the confusion about the nature of commitment is that any relationship can now be ended: divorce is easy. In this context, precisely what does it mean to have a committed relationship?

One can be committed in a free relationship, and one can be committed when the futurity is of the "ongoing" kind. What commitment means in this case is discussion and confrontation. When the conditions or feelings for one person in a committed "ongoing" relationship changes, one needs to tell the other what's happening. The main difference between a committed and an uncommitted relationship relates to this point.

In a committed relationship, you don't leave a note on the pillow saying, "Sorry, I'm leaving. I can't stand the.." (Fill in the blanks your own way.) Simply announcing why you intend to leave doesn't do it either. The realistic obligation in a relationship of this kind is talking about what's bothering you, in a way that the other person can hear, letting them know somehow, how crucially important the matter, the problem, or your feelings in this case are. Then, you need to give the other sufficient time to respond, to incorporate your distress and to adopt a solution if one is present. In that way you are giving your relationship a chance to adapt to changes in feelings, desires, and circumstances. A fuller discussion of this topic, how to confront in a relationship, is contained in Chapter XI.

Some relationships are intended to end. Many college relationships especially in the early college years have this underlying characteristic. They begin in September and they end in June. Tradionally, this was true until Senior year, when that relationship ended in marriage and a June wedding.

Time-Limited Relationships

Some established marriages are expected to dissolve when the children grow up and leave the nest. Travelers and tourists often take up with a native for the duration. In those cases, the sense of futurity may be different for the traveler and the local person, as in "Madame Butterfly."

Shifting futurity is not a simple matter, if one decides to change and extend the future. As in a brief encounter, what is acceptable, novel, pleasant, in a limited future may be intolerable and painful when it is seen as life entire. Bitterness can be overlooked in a long established relationship that is expected to end. The same bitterness may bar any renewed intimacy that a shift in futurity requires. Couples who have come to a mutual expectation that their relationship will end at some undefined point, often face this problem, when they have second thoughts about the end of their marriage.

Interestingly, futurity is different than the actual duration of a relationship. The futurity of a relationship is our expectation of its duration. The effect of this expectation can be positive or negative. Often marriages suffer from one spouse's expectation that now that they are married, they can do whatever they wish in the relationship: the other person is stuck. A relationship where there is less security may mean that the other is not "taken for granted." This can have a positive effect on a relationship. That means you must take other person's satisfaction into greater consideration; if not, the relationship may end. Different people respond differently to this important dimension of a relationship. Lack of a secure future may make others unable to relax and relate fully. Do you know yourself well enough to know which applies to you? How about your friend, what is her level of self knowledge?

Women in our culture frequently find it easier to be

in certain relationships in their 20's, knowing that this is not forever. Only as they face the end of appropriate child-bearing years may they feel it necessary to look for relationships that can last into old age. Dealing with this shift in futurity needs is often very painful. In some cases it means ending a somewhat enjoyable relationship: perhaps the man she is living with is unsuitable for the long term. In other instances, it means a shift in thinking, and a facing of actual instead of imagined values. What people find acceptable in their lives is often different from what they believe they somehow deserve, or ought to want.

For that reason, I usually advise people not to live with someone unless it's an open-ended relationship; i.e., has marriage as one possibility, or unless the relationship will have a automatic end to it. Getting out of a living arrangement that can only work temporarily is as painful emotionally as many divorces.

Forever Together

Traditionally, marriages in our culture have been established under the futurity of "In sickness and health, till death do us part." Such hopes remain strong, despite the current divorce statistics: approximately one out of two marriages end in divorce. I have yet to meet a divorced person who didn't experience the end of his marriage as a personal failure. Yet, in our fast-paced and ever changing culture, what other relationships remain constant? We rarely stay settled in other ways, why must we expect this one relationship to last when little else is permanent? On the other hand, it is easy to see how essential such a futurity was in earlier periods, when marriage was the principal support and refuge for an individual. Our culture is in a high and exciting place. This high spot allows many to have a extraordinary standard of personal freedom and growth based upon widespread economic well-being. The current fall off in the economy, which may be worse shortly, still leaves us in the developed western world with a material life unprecedented in history.

The personal freedom to arrange one's life, change lovers, occupations and amusements is traditionally the prerogative of ruling groups. In the past, only they, as a general rule, have had these priveleges. Occasionally, in Imperial cultures, as in Rome, a large stratum of a whole society becomes free enough from day to day worries over survival to change the cultural arrangements. Thus in Roman times as in ours, a weaker form of marriage became recognized, one not involving property to a significant extent.

Many people can not easily handle freedom; especially when appropriate culture structures are lacking. It is too soon for our culture to have evolved a changed institutional framework for the new developments in love relationships. The clearest new institution is that of "living together," still in its infancy. In past historical periods, only minorities were allowed the luxury of such social experimentation. Past experimental periods generally ended, when the decadent and pleasure loving rich were overwhelmed by the poor around them. We are in such a period of freedom. The knowledge explosion and new computer based methods of industrial and agricultural production promise much and may eventually free us all. Extensive, widespread leisure is a technical possibility for the first time, if we can also stop the explosive growth of population. Or we may become overwhelmed by the poverty stricken world about us in Asia, Latin-America and Africa.

The permanent marriage we have inherited from very recent generations is a survival institution. It is not based upon a long, healthy adult life, with personal growth and changes in interests. While divorce is now the frequent end of marriage, in the past, marriage often ended in widowhood, or was characterized by lengthy separations. Separations might last for years, or occur for most of the year for a lifetime. Permanent marriage is a security based institution, providing a relatively safe environment for the raising of children, the division of labor in the home economic unit, sex with responsibility for its inevitable products, children; care during illness; and a safe harbor during old age.

I had a patient who stayed years and years in a terrible marriage by most standards. The children were cared for and seemed OK. At first there was some minimal sex under unusual circumstances. The relationship was horrible, and I asked her why she stayed. "Well," she replied, "I grew up in Europe during the war and I know Karl could handle things helpfully, if something like that should happen again."

At the time I heard that I was shocked and horrified; but over the years of my practice I have seen similar security orientations underlying most long-term marriages. Years of experience affect people differently. The reasons for maintaining an attachment are often very unromantic.

A woman living home and raising children is affected so differently by life than her husband, travelling about and educating himself in far different ways. Why should their interests stay similar? The life experience of men and women in modern industrial society has been quite different until fairly recently. Now that more women enter the work force, there are indications that this may change. Still, how many women and men keep close friends of the same sex for over twenty five years? When there is a good sexual connection between man and wife that strengthens their bond; rarely does it remain so intensely pleasurable over a lifetime that it can continue to cement a relationship of two very distinct individuals.

A generation ago, the alternatives to an unhappy marriage were experienced as quite limited for many. When the number of divorced was low, those who divorced were seen as failures, and one's lifetime choice of a partner needed to be made at the choosing time: the time when all non-losers were present. Those who returned to play the game again were seen as failures. With so many millions now divorced, that can no longer act as a restraint. There is marriage after marriage, or even acceptable sexual lives for single people after marriage.

Much of this is evident to most people, although it is seldom put into words. Marriage requires so much encouragement that disparaging it is a felony, a positive danger to the social fabric. Yet it is clear with these great social changes, that the pledge "...in sickness and health, till death do us part" has a small relationship to the current American experience. Beginning marriage with the idea that it must be forever makes the choice of a partner a difficult one, for what else lasts forever in our culture? We live in a world of constant freedom to choose and rechoose our partners. No longer do the bulk of the marriageable make their choice in a narrow age period. Marriage can be put off indefinitely until the exact right one comes along; until then there is the choice of all the millions who read the personal columns. There is the ever present danger of getting stuck with the wrong choice and then...failure.

To me, a more limited futurity, say of two to five years, makes more sense in this context. While I am not recommending a precise contract, I think that the idea that a marriage not forever is a failure is often destructive. As people change, marriages need to be renegotiated, if possible. The idea that a marriage should continue indefinitely no matter what, frightens many people and makes the institution seem disadvantageous in the medium time-span for many. The most vivid example of this in my mind came from the case of a young physician. A resident in a charity hospital, his working hours were long. He was very conscientious and devoted himself to his patients. He had become involved with a beautiful woman he had met on the Emergency Ward. At that time Greta had a drug problem.

Conscientious Rick was her white knight. He saw her through her drug problem and lived with her for several years. Now, faced with marriage, he focused on two minor blemishes to Greta's considerable beauty. I was unable to figure out what lay beneath his excuses.

One day he asked me, "Do you think that I'll ever sleep with another woman besides Greta?" Unclear about his issues, I didn't answer him at first.

The same question came up again, repeatedly, at other sessions. Finally I answered him: "I think it's unlikely that Greta is the only woman you'll ever have sex with."

He was furious. "Then why bother marrying?" He admitted attractions to other women. I pointed out to him that he could be monogamous if he wished, I was merely noting the statistics.

Evidently his wishes weren't very strong, for that remark wasn't reassuring. I again pointed out to Rick that my reply was statistical for men in his social class, and included the possibilities of widowhood and divorce, but his bubble was burst. In a fury he left me. Without the assurance of a permanent marriage, the whole institution seemed pointless. Yet, he himself found such an arrangement imprisoning. He obsessed about a mole that marred the beauty of a woman he said he loved, rather than face his feelings of confinement in a monogamous marriage.

For Rick, like many others, marriage could only mean forever. When you have such a belief system, you will find it hard to continue a good relationship, once you realize that it may end. You might do better with a more limited futurity. An example is the following proposal: "Let's get married and have children, and then, when the kids get into school, we'll see where we are at." Such relationships might last a lifetime, or their ending could be done more easily, with the spouses not lulled into a false sense of permanence. That expectation of permanence often means that people neglect their employability and attractiveness. Of course, if they didn't neglect their employability and attractiveness they might stay married.

7
When Children Are There

Developing a relationship when children are present in your life or your significant other's life is much a different game. Not only must you both consider others, these others may be more important to your wanted other than you are. Many men find it hard to adjust to their wives' new and principal interest when a baby is born: how much more difficult some find the adjustment when the children are not entering an already solid relationship between man and wife, but are there first.

Many good women will say, "I love him, but not more than my son." Many good men look around for a woman who will help with the care of their children from a previous marriage. This man is secretly or openly looking for a high level housekeeper; yet he will devote less to his helper and lover than he would to paid help...in money at least. Not terribly important for her own sake, and underpaid from a work standpoint, no wonder this woman is dismayed.

While many parents see the needs of their children as primary, others give lip service to the importance of their children and in fact use them to hide their own mixed feelings about a new involvement. Parents feel more secure in their relationship with their children than they do with a new relationship. Often a single child will become in fact the "significant other" for an adult single parent.

Observing the breakup and remarriage of a successful consulting engineer, I watched an unambivalent wife and mother pursue and remarry. She had decided that she wanted Joe somewhat before he had really faced the dissolution of his marriage. Denice separated from her own husband and moved into a motel. Joe quickly followed her out of his house and into that single room, home to her and her children.

"This is Joseph," said Denice, to her son and daughter. "He is very important to me. Please be nice to him. I love him deeply. If you don't think you want to be nice to him, you can live with your father."

When Joe talked to me later about this moment from his past, he was very moved. "...and as a result, I've had quite a good relationship with both of them, and I'm quite involved in their lives."

Looking about him, at his friends who had also divorced and remarried, Joe felt quite lucky. Creating a new family from the shreds of an old one is extremely difficult. Modest ambitions are important. The new father or mother is often struggling to be included in the family that has existed before him.

Denice's remarks may seem too extreme for some. For other people they are simply untrue; children are more important to them. It is important to recognize that Denice was saying to her children that if they were unreasonable they would become less important, not that she didn't want or love them.

Her new family has been successful. She did make the relationship with Joe primary in the way that relationships are usually primary between husband and wife. She faced her internal priorities.

Observing another couples' struggle to combine their children and themselves into one family, I could see the wisdom of Denice and Joe's method. This method is only workable when the parents do have a strong basic interest in children. Otherwise the children will think that their parents are not simply insisting on a reasonable attitude; instead they will feel abandoned.

Henry and Karen were both quite child oriented school teachers, each with three children. They recognized that combining households would be a major task; but each looked forward to the time when someone could be an additional parent to their children. For themselves, they wanted someone to share their life, and the complex, exasperating, fulfilling activities of parenthood.

Henry's children knew that they had the upper hand with their father, as did everyone else in the joint household. Perhaps that is the way it should be. In practice it had unfortunate consequences.

Karen had complaints about Henry's daughter. "She refuses to help me with the dishes. She says yes and does nothing," Karen claimed.

Henry listened carefully to Karen, and did nothing. Not quite nothing, even Karen would admit that he didn't do absolutely nothing. For instance, he told Karen how much he loved her, and he promised to take care of the matter. Not only did he not take care of the matter, he avoided taking his wife out alone. He would stop at a fancy restaurant and bring food home instead. He wanted to include his kids. Dinner meant dinner with the whole family at home; still he didn't want Karen to work too hard. He kept telling Karen how much he loved her and how important she was to him.

Throughout his marriage to Karen, Henry's children and Karen both knew that Karen was the less important. Early on her marriage to Henry, his children threatened her.

"We've gotten rid of Dad's girl friends before," said the youngest in an angry fight.

Of course this relationship, this marriage, finally collapsed. Observing this from the outside it seemed that two incidents crystalized the eventual failure of their relationship in Karen's mind. First in one of their last fights, Karen asked Henry once again, "Do something, for God's sake about your daughter's attitude. She just won't help in the kitchen."

"You're quite right Karen," he said, "and next time she does it, you just let me know."

Then one of Karen's children got in trouble with the police. Henry was leaning towards letting the law take its course. Karen thought he was being quite impossible, (although her son was more impossible). Especially after all that she had done for his children. Their marriage ended.

Neither Henry nor Karen would acknowledge that their adolescent children were more important to them than each other. The disappointment Karen felt seemed to revolve around this point. Yet the same was true for her. Their relationship might have had a chance if Henry acknowledged the relatively greater importance of his children to her, especially since that was really true for her as well. Perhaps they ought to have preserved separate households, as more truly reflecting the state of their relationships.

Really Wanting To Be Number One

With great hopes comes great disappointments. In our culture, marriage is often seen as the "Final and Total Solution to Life's Problems." Many people express the idea that they will get in this relationship all that they have always longed for. Being the most important person to someone came high on the list for Frank. He longed for complete and total intimacy with another, but he chose as his second wife a strong conscientious woman, very connected to her role as a mother.

Frank had certainly expected to be important to Tilly, not realizing that Tilly's daughter by her previous marriage was of primary importance to her. If the house was burning, she would certainly think of her daughter first; Frank would be an afterthought. That's the sort of thing that many couples who have jointly conceived or adopted a child would do. But Frank had always longed to be number one. He liked children, wanted some himself, tried to be nice to his wife's child, but he had terrible attacks of jealous rage, alternating with fits of sulking.

Surprisingly, Frank himself had a step-father, and knew the difficulties of that relationship from the child's side. Still, marriage had meant to him that he would be first, at last.

Men often have this problem with their own biological children, for the coming of a child naturally means less attention for them. Whatever Frank's intellectual understanding of the issues, he became increasingly upset as he understood that his life was constantly interrupted by the needs of his wife's daughter.

Perhaps Tilly's first husband sensed the problem. He made things difficult from the beginning. He changed his mind about baby-sitting for the honeymoon. Tilly wouldn't settle for a last minute unknown baby-sitter. No honeymoon!

Tilly needed to talk to her ex-husband from time to time about their daughter and the custody of her that they shared. Frank and Tilly were both often thrown off balance by the suddenness of the meetings. Tilly's relationship with her ex-husband was never very good. It had become more difficult after her divorce. Frank had terrible attacks of jealousy whenever she spent time with her domineering ex-husband. Tilly was so wonderful, he was sure her husband wanted her back.

Frank became severely depressed in the second year of his marriage. At first he couldn't understand himself. Why was he unhappy? This was his best relationship. Yet, in this best relationship he had ever had, he felt both insecure and second in importance.

Fortunately, he was able to accept this unpleasant realization, and preserve his marriage. I say "fortunately", because he had many good things on an "adult basis" from his wife: caring companionship, loyalty, a sexual relationship that was fulfilling at times, and a person to help him create a home. The need to be absolutely central to another person was not fulfilled in his marriage, however.

To many psychologists, that intense need we feel in a passionate love relationship comes from another place, another time, another relationship. That feeling we may have had that our life absolutely depends on being central to another person makes sense as the feelings of an infant. An infant's life truly depends on being central to his mother, or so it was in primitive society when we evolved, and that remains the infant's experience. Many of our wishes for and in an adult love relationship are carry-overs from an unfulfilled childhood. Seeing someone else's child, or even our own, get these from the person who is central to our own desire can be especially painful.

Questions To Ask Yourself

1. Who is more important to you, your children or your lover? Who will be more important in five years? Can you discuss this openly?

2. Do you expect your lover to do more parenting for you than you for him/her?

8
Marriage or Living Together

A student of mine was visited by a master of the Sufi order, a mystic.

"What do the Sufis believe?" he asked.

"One hundred years ago they were concerned about some things, now they are concerned about other things," answered the master.

Few spokesmen for institutions are so frank about real changes that occur behind names that stay the same. Marriage today occurs in a social context much different than one hundred years ago, or even fifty years ago when many Americans were still farmers. Small town environments were home to another large fraction of the population. Marriage occurred during a fairly narrow age span for most people. Labor saving devices for the home weren't nearly as widespread as now. The meaning of choosing marriage or of living together has changed radically. One hundred years ago there were some people who chose to live together. A few artists and bohemians defied convention. Other social outcasts ignored the social rules, as is always true. But something is markedly different in a society when many people make a specific decision. What was once an isolating or heroic or painful decision, has become an ordinary choice for many people.

Technological change has altered the setting, the context, the need that marriage fulfills. One hundred years ago only the rich could afford a complete and organized household catering to one person; therefore society organized itself around other options. Today, a single person with a moderate income can arrange for his own shelter, cooking, health care, and amusement without needing to participate in a family or other complicated living arrangement.

Only a couple of generations ago the majority of women were economically dependent on their fathers, husbands, and brothers. They certainly worked hard enough, but they played a small and brief role in the public, cash economy. Now the majority of women work both before and after marriage. The role of male provider is no longer central to the structure of marriage.

Sex and Technology

Technology has even revolutionized sexual life. What was once a private act is now shown in great detail on the movie screen. Sex is pictured and described in a thousand books, books that were once the rare delight of wealthy collectors. Detailed surveys are available that allow each person to monitor and compare his sexual activity to others. Measurements are available of the average size of sexual organs. Sex has changed from being an intensely private, almost reflexive activity to a semi-public, quantifiable and comparable one. Masturbation has been revolutionized. This has always been the permanently available outlet for the socially and economically disadvantaged, and the occasional choice for many. For some it has been the preferred choice. Richard Burton, the 19th century explorer and the famous translator of the Arabian Nights was also known in Victorian society as a sexual adventurer. Still, the following rhyme is attributed to him.

For pleasure, Japanese women
For variety, Indian women
For joy, an Afghan boy
But for ecstasy, a Persian melon

Mechanical sex-dolls are made to fit male needs, but the important beneficiaries of technical advance in mechanical sex are women. The vibrator provides superior orgasms for many women. So much so, that vibrator addiction is a substantial clinical problem. One patient of mine, a successful professional woman, had to get rid of the vibrator before she had the energy to pursue a relationship. It was not that she preferred men to her mechanical toy from a sexual point of view. She valued the pleasure her vibrator gave her. She did however want the whole relationship package.

Modern culture however doesn't make the whole package necessary. In a traditional relationship everything was included in the relationship willy-nilly. The partialing out that is possible in our society was unknown. We who are exposed to excellence in a number of fields and who analyze everything, can dream of an "ideal" mate as having the maximum quantity of our values from "a to z." Our greedy consciousness creates composite ideals unfillable by mortals. The technical perfection of our records and movies is possible by splicing moments of perfection. The exciting records we listen to are often put together by splicing five minute sections, well and separately rehearsed. Similarly , in our present culture it is possible to actually put together a relational life in a similar fashion: some sex from our girl friend Linda, companionship from Mary, our bright and energetic fellow worker, and deep understanding from Joan, the girl we met in group therapy. All the while we share in the joys of parenting with our ex-wife Tilly - or try to.

Technology has made autonomy possible, at least in the short run. Technology has also made having children a voluntary decision in the developed world. Throughout the urban parts of the United States, and to a lesser degree, urban Western Europe, it is now possible to live alone comfortably. Large numbers of single people can afford a decent place of their own, not a room in someone else's house. Micro-wave cooking, television, computer games, the telephone, and low-cost transportation have all added to the lower attractive power of the family for many people. Certain pornographic or sexually stimulating literature can provide a powerful substitute for the presence of an actual person, like the centerfold of Playboy or Playgirl magazine.

Possibly more important, now that single adults are available in large numbers throughout a broad age range, the whole social world has changed. No longer do people stay in marriages with the certainty that outside of a bad marriage there is only a world of relationally incompetent singles: people with something wrong, losers. "He's never been married," was a clear indication of pathology a generation ago. Divorce indicated something worse.

Any discussion of choosing marriage requires us to face the fact that the word marriage means many different arrangements. We are actually now in the cultural situation of there being two forms of marriage, the strong form which we call marriage, and a weaker form not involving property rights usually called living together. Certainly "living together" involves public recognition and acceptance of sexual co-habitation.

Marriages vary so much that on any single dimension there may be more differences amongst married people than there are between married and non-married people. Certainly some married people spend less time with each other actually conversing than many singles who are merely dating. Many established marriages are characterized by minimal (once a month) or non-existent sexual relationships.

Living together has a poor reputation now among many of the marriage minded, especially women. The problem, as far as I understand it, is that many women seem to have entered into living together arrangements with the idea that these arrangements would remain, or become permanent. They then gave too much of themselves in the hope of a deferred return. When the relationship turned disappointing, and ended, they felt cheated.

Most relationships become disappointing: the honeymoon ends. At that point every relationship undergoes a transition. Either it is renegotiated without many of the illusions and hopes that accompanied its creation, or it ends completely. The first time this happens is usually the most painful. Not everyone has this experience; some marry with minimal expectations. That transition, that renegotiation when the honeymoon is over, is easier inside the socially supported marriage bond. Simply walking off in disappointment is too difficult for most married people; with delay, a new and satisfactory relationship may be worked out. This new relationship exists without a formal announcement, it is a shift in private understandings. All long term relationships have to shift; no two people stay exactly the same, or change in the same manner.

Because marriage has a longer futurity, there is a greater commitment to work at such shifts. The futurity in living together is often different: "We'll stay together as long as it is convenient." It is possible to make the futurity different in living together: "Living together will be OK with me, as long as you agree that we'll sincerely try to make our relationship work and last." When living together ends, whatever the futurity has been, the ending is as painful as divorce. Our attachments seem to be a function of the intertwining of our lives, more than the expectations and plans we made at their beginning. The lack of an extended futurity, and the lack of social support and pressure for staying together, are forces that make it harder to renegotiate a new relationship outside the marriage bond.

It is common for me to hear talk about people's, or especially, men's difficulty in committing themselves to a marriage oriented relationship. Important understanding of the current world is avoided by simply blaming men, or women who "can't commit themselves." Why should people commit themselves for a lifetime when everyone knows that the exciting part of a relationship is destined to end in a few years? When one examines the social pressure that has helped marriages stay together it must be obvious that if marriages stayed always desirable, it wouldn't be necessary to pressure people to stay in them.

Once the psychological leap is made to considering living together as a weaker form of marriage, it should be even more clear that the marriage bond is intended to be less inclusive and permanent than before. Most people seem to dislike thinking of themselves as being married many times. Living together provides a low-risk alternative. One can "marry" and fail without counting the failure as marriage.

A theme of this book is awareness. Facing oneself and the hidden bases of one's activity is the key to good relationships. Why then do I include this long discussion of cultural change in a chapter on marriage? I am convinced that the principal reasons people continue to marry are not clear to them. There is tremendous romanticism and self-deception here. Only by facing what marriages are and can be, can one really choose a workable model for oneself.

Advantages of Marriage

Marriage seems very attractive for women concerned about how their beauty fades, and men who believe their future prospects are poor, including soldiers who fear dying tomorrow. Most people are still concerned over "bastardy" and therefore usually choose marriage when children are involved. The problem of getting married becomes more complicated when both man and woman don't want children. Society has a vested interest in raising children well, and supports the nuclear family on that basis. When there are no children involved, society's interest is much weaker.

There is certain statistical evidence that men who marry live longer and healthier lives than those who don't. My observation of the average single life and satisfaction shows more average satisfaction amongst married people, although there are so many individual differences that I see these figures as a poor guide to any particular person's decision.

It seems appropriate to me that I should say something about my own life in this area, so as not to make the gulf between my public pronouncements and private life too wide. I still enjoy a marriage of twenty years, despite my many unromantic remarks. I am often seen as a difficult and demanding person by others, and they are probably right. I wouldn't have stayed in many of the marriages I see. When we married, neither my wife nor I secretly expected our marriage to last, although neither of us said that to each other. Partially as a result of that expectation, we have been able to change our relationship as our needs changed. We have two children who are very important to us. We have had stormy fights now and then; at the same time we have been supportive of any strongly felt need of the other. This synergistic attitude has made negotiations worthwhile.

Currently, in the United States, the economic merging that occurs in marriage adds considerably to many people's material life. Two can not live as cheaply as one, but two incomes are better than one. Two incomes add greatly to economic security. A new group of high-income couples have developed where both husband and wife have well-paying jobs.

Marriage "until death us do part", of course, makes sense when you have found the perfect person who indubitably will make you happy under any and all circumstances for the rest of your life, no matter how you change, and for whom you too can be perfect under all circumstances. Commitment becomes more difficult under less ideal circumstances. This is so much more true today, when the pool of eligible mates apparently continues to be full for many years longer than in the past. The awareness of constant potential for change, for a new partner, has an effect on existing relationships. Choosing to live together makes sense when there is a clear mutual understanding about what is involved, what futurity is intended. Writing things down helps, not because contracts are legally binding, but because it reminds people of what they said, both before and after saying them.

The greatest disadvantage of living together seems to come from the pain and disappointment when the relationship "fails." Of course, whether or not the relationship has failed depends on your futurity, your initial expectations of its duration. Theoretically, rationally, the ending of living together ought to be easier to handle than a divorce. Sometimes it is.

In cases like Mitch's, separation has been very hurtful. Mitch decided to live with Jane when he didn't want to face losing her after dating her for a year. She wanted the relationship to "go somewhere". They moved into a nice house. Each had high hopes and great suspicions. While wishing that the relationship would develop, neither would invest very much of themselves, not trusting the other's seriousness. Mitch wanted a rather traditional wife, someone to cook and cater to him. Jane thought that was pointless when she had to tend to her career. Jane wanted Mitch to help her financially with her education, but Mitch felt that the stock market was a better investment, especially as he wasn't expecting their relationship to last. He was right, their relationship didn't last. If he had helped her more (she had to drop out of school), or if she had cared for him more, I think their relationship would have endured.

Since their split up they haven't established much in the way of serious relationships. Mitch especially has had a hard time genuinely putting his energy in a new relationship. He didn't want to fail, so he held back in the first place. His holding back, his low energy investment has gotten worse since he has become more fearful.

One can see, in his process, two of the principal problems in "living together". Lack of a high energy commitment leads to failure, and the pain of the relationship not working out bruises the particapants quite seriously. While adult sexual life batters and bruises very severely many of its participants, we are better prepared to face this in an actual divorce. Few seem prepared to deal with the magnitude of disappointment and hurt that often result after living together. Without the social support that the pain of divorce gains, these feelings are more often swept out of awareness, reducing the pain, perhaps, but increasing the mischief such pain causes. The excessively long futurity of the traditional marriage seems a poor match for modern conditions, but living together has its own severe problems.

There are large individual differences in reaction to being married. More than one colleague has reported having patients who have suddenly become sexually unwilling after marriage, a change from before. For others, being married is a license to take advantage of one's trapped spouse. Something like the "tenure" system at universities, there are those who stop producing once they're guaranteed a job.

The long futurity of "Until death do us part" has a positive effect on some people's relationships. Many people still gain an extended family and support system, a pleasant addition in some cases. Others find it a great pain to have to associate with those with whom one has no basis in common interest for a relationship. "The worst tyranny" said an old German philosopher, "is to have to associate with blood relations." The social pressure against dissolving relationships still often has a positive effect in carrying couples through momentary bad periods.

Although there are many critics of the nuclear and extended family, no clear alternative seems to have developed that has the stability of blood relations or marriage. Should you be interested in marriage in either the weak (living together) or conventional form, do the following. Spend time talking about your expectations in different areas. Sex and Money are the areas of great marital difficulty. Consider using your courtship period to work those areas through, at least initially.

Try not to marry with the idea that it is determinedly forever. Work hard to improve your marriage, to make it satisfactory. Exhaust the possibilities of counseling, of experiment, but be prepared to end your marriage after a number of bad years. A lifetime of bitterness does no one any good. Unless of course you are simply a miserable, bitter person. Then, if your bitterness is not really the consequence of your marriage, you might enjoy your miserable years better if you can persuade your spouse to stay with you.

This is probably a good place to discuss criteria for divorce. A workable procedure for deciding on divorce is as follows. Look about you. Remember that the two independent areas crucial to your marriage are your sexual life and your economic life. If they are good, significantly above the average of your friends, don't divorce. Accept the limitations of your marriage for it's doubtful that you can do better. If both areas (sex and money) are bad or below average seriously consider divorce. You can probably do better with someone else.

The hardest decisions about divorce come when sex is good and money is bad, or vice versa. In fact, these are the cases I more often see in treatment, since at least one partner generally recognizes that work at improvement makes most sense under these circumstances.

Questions To Help Both Of You Decide

Write down what you will do if there is a pregnancy, what you will do with any jointly bought property, how long you intend to "try it together." Use this document to clear up your thinking. Is this a free relationship, or a trial marriage? Face the economic aspects of your choice squarely. Hopefully you can both benefit. Face also the fact that separation will be difficult. Think of how you would like to handle a possible separation ahead of time. A period of notice, or an adjustment period for separation will help. In any case, discussing these issues ahead of time will make your relationship clearer.

9
Children: To Have or Have Not

Expectations about having children are central to the relationship of a young man and woman. A generation or two ago this was hardly a matter of conscious choice. The improvement and continuation of the race through procreation was considered by some nineteenth century philosophers to be man's main task; thus elevating and sanctifying an almost universal experience. Now when childbearing is an area of relatively easy choice through birth control, the possibility of having a family extending through time still creates the context for marriage.

Modern culture allows us to separate and analyze wholes that once were inseparable. The telephone allows friendship to continue over distance in ways that were unthinkable generations ago. As recently as the 1950's a popular song said that "...Love and marriage go together like a horse and carriage."

Only a few generations ago, sexual pleasure was generally considered as relatively unimportant, especially for women, and there was always a place in the extended family for those who didn't marry. Thus companionship needs and the division of labor were handled. Birth control was more difficult and expensive, as it still is in the underdeveloped countries. On a farm, a child's labor becomes useful early. In that milieu, those couples who chose not to have children were looked on as selfish, not wanting to contribute to the human race. Now of course, with the world's overpopulation, that argument, as so many others for the having of children, is no longer valid. With 5 billion people on the planet not having children is arguably a positive social good. Certainly arguments against celibacy and homo-sexuality lose their force in this context.

If however the world has too many children, it certainly doesn't have too many well educated rational and competent adults. No one who responsibly wishes to raise a child need worry about harm to the race by adding a person. Still, all of these changes make the decision more personal and individual.

In this, as in so many other aspects of having a relationship, much trouble comes from assuming that what is common is universal. Not every woman is very maternal, or wishes to devote a large part of her life to child-raising. This is especially true in a culture like ours that doesn't value and reward motherhood highly. Not every man feels very protective of the woman he loves, to the point of marrying her when she gets pregnant. (It is worth noting that getting pregnant in Sweden for many women has been the only way to move their relationships to marriage. In that culture, perhaps a more advanced form of our own, with little social pressure against pre-marital sex, there often is apparently little other incentive to marry for many couples. In the United States too I have observed couples living together until a child was due; then marriage seemed appropriate.)

It is important to explore with your other, what they are really wanting in their life, and what they will accept. It is a good method in all your negotiations with a friend: find out what is their minimum requirement and their maximum hope in each area of their life. Then inspect your own wishes and needs and find the overlapping area that gives you both the most. Thus if she wants at least one child, and would love four while you would prefer to be childless for the next seven years, but might like to have a child or two eventually, you likely could agree to have one child in a few years and then see where you are "at".

Of course this seems obvious. The difficult part is knowing yourself and exposing your wishes and needs. For the possibility is that they will lead to your rejection.

Although sudden, possibly premature, marriage as a result of pregnancy guarantees misery for many, yet sometimes it works. Ironically, I have seen a couple concerned about not being "ready", give up the child, only to remarry and miss it later!

Often the choice not to have children is made on economic grounds. It is important to note how mixed the data bearing on that decision. Married family men on the whole seem to be motivated to work harder and make more money than other men. This has been part of the reason for married men being a preferred part of the labor force; while on the contrary, the demands of being a mother often take a woman out of the labor force and back home, which has contributed to lower wages for women.

Is there any basis for a rational, somewhat skeptical person to choose to have children in the present context? Certainly having children and being a good parent is now akin to a hobby in many ways, perhaps the most expensive hobby around. In a world with many possibilities for travel, personal development and adventure, having a child restricts one's possibilities.

Yet, watching her childless aunt slowly end alone in an old-folks' home propelled one thirty-five year old woman into marriage and child-birth. Even if social security and other insurance plans take care of the economic needs of the aged, the lack of children and grandchildren provides little automatic participation in the world as one gets older. Child rearing is an expensive form of old-age insurance, but one that has few substitutes. Social critics of the family have been unable to come up yet with substitutes that have staying power. In northwest Arkansas, where I occasionally do a workshop, there were many communes in the late '60s and '70s, encouraged by the cheap land prices. Only one remains, and that is subsidized by a land trust. Even so, the family as a solution to the emotional problems of old age often fails in America. Parents often are unable to develop children who wish to have anything to do with their aging parents.

We are closer to children than to any animal species. Yet animals as pets certainly can be more loving. A trip to the pet cemetery certainly demonstrates where some people have found love. Children provide less love, more challenge and travail for many. Yet the stability of marriage requires joint projects. Children may not be the joint project for your relationship, but without some joint projects ordinary developments take people apart.

I still note that convention rules for many deciding to have children. Although I say this, I feel especially fortunate in my own family. Perhaps this has given me the perspective to see that the choice to have children is often not justifiable on rational grounds. The balance of pleasure and pain in many families should have certainly dictated against a rational choice to have children.

At the same time, I feel very aware that those whom I've observed choosing not to have them seem to have no more in the long run. Those careful calculators who felt that they could do better without them, actually often end up with less, emotionally and spiritually. Having children is an incentive to work and accumulate.

After mentioning all these arguments, do I have any advice to offer?

Before advice, I have a perspective. The basis on which much child rearing has existed no longer exists. Many individuals and couples can choose to not have children in the current context.

If you're not terribly keen on having them, not having them is probably the better idea. Childrearing requires too much energy to be undertaken casually. If after hearing my suggestion for a decision "rule", you still can't decide, then follow tradition, which after all represents some distillation of what has worked for many.

10
Monogamy and Its Alternatives

The monogamous ideal is powerful in our culture, yet our private behavior seems much different. More than half of the married men have reported affairs, in surveys, for some time. The proportion of younger women who are sexually active outside of marriage has been increasing, approaching the male level in certain groups. In our thinking, however, this behavior is always unusual, exceptional. The goal of this chapter is simply to open your consciousness to considerations of monogamy's limitations, as well as some of the problems with its alternatives, in our contemporary world. Rarely do we fully consider these issues as rational, personal, and social alternatives. Yet the ideal of monogamy is more breached than honored; perhaps these deviations have their own logic.

In the biblical account of creation, God says to Adam "I will make you a help meet for you... so you will be like one flesh." Despite the monogamous ideal, the early patriarchs are reported to have more than one woman. Sarah had her maidservant Hagar conceive for her when she herself was barren. The Muslim culture is still polygamous, as are many other cultures. In practice this means that more successful men can have more than one established and publicly recognized relationship. Adultery was still punished in the biblical period, which meant in practice that men were entitled to more sexual variety and freedom than women.

Differences Between Men and Women

Cultures where women have several husbands exist, but are comparatively rare. In one Indian culture women have several husbands, but the meaning seems different than in male polygamy. In that small tribe, several brothers, or close friends, pool their resources to share one wife. Thus we have little evidence that women have the same widely distributed need for a multiplicity of partners that men have shown, male fantasies to the contrary. Those male fantasies more often reflect male projection: men imagining that their girl friends want to do what men secretly wish for themselves.

Studies of animal sexual behavior and characteristics largely support the idea of certain widespread biological sexual differences. In this controversial area, I will begin by quoting the authority of the Encyclopedia Brittanica, which has a rather poetic statement on the subject: "The great claw of the fiddler crab, the antlers of a moose, the great bulk and strength of a harem master in a fur seal colony, the beautiful fan tail of the peacock, and the bright feathers of other birds, are all distinctively male characteristics, and all are associated with the sexual drive of males. Females, by and large, are of comparatively quiet disposition and a relatively drab appearance. Their function is to produce and nurture eggs, as safely and usually as inconspicuously as possible. The male function is to find and fertilize the female, for which both drive and display are generally required. It is the business of sperm to be active and so find an egg. Similarly it is the business of males to find a female and mate with her if possible. The male drive, or male eagerness, is a consequence of this special function of males."

Comparing the sexual activities of male and female homosexuals is another source of data on differences in sexual activity and need between men and women. Here again, widespread differences appear between male and female. The male homosexual culture is on the whole characterized by more sexual activity with more and different partners. The female homosexual world has been known, in recent time, for relatively stable connections. That culture has a greater relationship focus than the male homosexual world.

The arguments that there are widespread differences in sexual behavior between men and women need to be used very cautiously. Such arguments have been misused badly in the past to add to the oppression of women, and to a lesser extent, men. You will be on much safer ground your life will be much more successful, if you pay more attention to your inner needs, than to cultural patterns and statistical averages. That is one more reason to stress knowing yourself. Averages and group patterns are weak guides to what we can expect from ourselves and others; they should never be used as strait jackets. It is also important to recognize that our cultural choice for monogamy is somewhat distinctive, perhaps even unusual in the history of mankind. This choice may be a somewhat heavier burden for males than females. Again, borrowing from the authority of the Encyclopedia Brittanica: "Human beings are not inherently monogamous but have a natural desire for diversity in their sexuality as in other aspects of life."

Monogamy's Disadvantages

In understanding alternatives to monogamy, remember the wide differences between people. Not everyone's reasons are the same. Sexual boredom and a desire for variety is more important for those people who have had everything, or at least, a lot of everything. Lack of sexual fulfillment, misunderstanding between spouses, a loss of general intimacy are other reasons that make physical intimacy emotionally inappropriate. Habitual or extended separation makes finding another partner simply a natural reaction for some people.

Many women have come to the conclusion that their sex has been somehow cheated by society in general. They follow the general rule: Do whatever men have always done. This is their personal solution to end their oppression. Many males chafe under their probably biological drives for sexual diversity and expansion: certainly men who are rich enough, or free enough have tended to take more than one woman. Women who are without interest in children often find themselves drawn to a freer sexual life.

Currently we are formally monogamous, which means for us, serial monogamy, or a series of ostensibly monogamous relationships, for many people. Divorce is not terribly difficult, although almost universally painful. "Living together" has developed as a weaker form of marriage, with less mutual responsibilities, minimal economic sharing, and a weak sense of the future. Presumably this makes the pain of separation less. Certainly people don't have to count such relationships as failed marriages, which seems to be a blessing to some.

Nonetheless woman are once again apparently at the short end of the cultural arrangement. Divorced women who are heads of families, that is to say, mothers living with their children, have been described as the largest poverty-stricken group in the United States. They typically receive only minimal child support or alimony.

The children of divorced families also are deprived in various ways, although the economic criteria are easiest to measure. There are such differences among families that it is hard to generalize about the emotional effects of divorce. That it is an economic disaster for many is clear. Certainly the emotional effects on children who grow up in angry and unhappy families have been documented many times. When the economic aspects of the family are good, and the emotional aspects are bad, women have a hard time deciding about continuing their marriages.

Because of the high premium on youth and physical attractiveness for woman—and homosexuals—age is no blessing for single woman and homosexuals. Heterosexual men clearly have more opportunities as they age, provided they demonstrate economic viability. Thus it is not clear that serial monogamy has been an unmixed advance for women, generally the strongest and most vociferous upholders of monogamous life. The present arrangement does not necessarily serve certain groups of women well. Many women in the United States would clearly have been better off in a system that allowed for a less restrictive marriage that would allow their husbands a larger degree of sexual freedom, while still encouraging their husbands' participation in their family life. In some ways, joint custody is a step in this direction. I have also noticed, among some of my patients, that men and women still return to be lovers, especially in the situation where divorce occurs among older couples. A man may create new liaisons, often with younger women, but his previous wife may find it still convenient, for a variety of reasons, to maintain some sort of sexual connection. (This is such a taboo subject that I have not seen it discussed anywhere, although it's existence is not so uncommon.)

Polyandrous cultures, where women have as much sexual freedom as men, are rare, as mentioned earlier. Their existence, however, demonstrates something about human possibility for that minority of women who are adventurous and ambitious for the same kinds of sexual freedoms that many men have historically enjoyed.

Another important cultural development making monogamy less appealing has been improved life expectancy. Both women and men are living longer, and early widowhood is much less common. Long-lasting relationships were not so universal when the death rate was higher. The longer life-span facing relationships has made imperfect relationships less attractive to many.

I am not recommending a return to the double

standard. I am recommending increased open-minded-
ness, knowledge of your own limits, and flexibility in
making your own arrangements. Tradition is a weak
force in modern industrial society at present. Each
person must work out his own relationship, with much
less social support, or automatic agreement from his
partner. It is helpful to find social support, or like-
minded individuals, but the responsiblity for working
out a sexual life falls much greater on the individual
now.

If your mind has been opened to the recognition
that monogamy and sexual exclusivity aren't the only
decent and natural solutions, what are the alternatives?
Are there any reasonable guidelines or directives in this
area?

Here, as in so many aspects of relationships,
understanding yourself, understanding what is really
important to you, is central. A young biologist told me
recently of a conversation she had with her boyfriend.
She was returning to a specimen gathering expedition
for about a month. He told her that he wanted her to
promise not to do anything sexual while she was away.

After about a month he changed his position. "I
realize," he said, "that what is most important to me is
that you'll come back. If I tell you that you can't do
anything, you'll probably do it just to show that you're a
free person."

He was able to realize that he had little likelihood of
being able to control someone's sexual behavior when
there was a substantial absence. What happens under
those conditions is a function of the person's habits,
moods, and opportunities. He was also able to recognize

what was important to him in the situation: his girlfriend's full return to him. Insecurity over the possible loss of a lover was his main concern, arranging for security in one's primary relationship is crucial in having non-tumultuous affairs. Those mates who accept this seem relatively certain that they won't lose what they have to another. This allows them to be accepting of their partners need for a degree of freedom.

"Swinging" or wifeswapping was particularly designed to control that anxiety. The hope for swingers has frequently been that in such controlled sexual adventures, no one would get carried away sexually and emotionally. Also, equality would prevail and guilt would be eliminated. The insecurity generated by both partners constantly experimenting with different lovers seems more than even the most experimental relationship can stand for long.

One problem that has afflicted swingers is that men have great sexual fantasies of indefinite performance, while women, who often fantasize less, have the capacity to do more. Often men who would drag their unwilling ladies to swinging parties as the price of their own admittance, and free emotional participation, have discovered that their shy feminine companions learned to function better than hoped for under the circumstances! Women have a greater physiological capacity for multiple and rapidly repeating sexual functioning than men. It is hard to predict the outcome of such adventures.

John, the lover of the biologist off to collect specimens, needs to believe he is very important to his girl friend, or that he will be lucky, or that she will be determined to return to him no matter what pleasures and men she encounters. Her protestation that she has taken a long time between affairs wouldn't reassure many men. That long gap in time probably reflects the painful aftermath of her last affair: her grief and pain over loss, and the blow to her self-esteem in her failure. Knowing that she can count on her lover and feeling loved, she may be much more open to a new adventure. Still, I am impressed by their self-knowledge and their relationship has a better chance at succeeding than many. You cannot demand fidelity of a person when you are not present.

At the opposite extreme, mixing two lovers on the same territory is very difficult. The movie "Shampoo" illustrated this problem, when one of the chief characters brought his wife and mistress to the same party. Many women are apparently willing to accept their husbands' affairs as long as they don't have to share the same territory, or deal with their actual presence. The arrangement in "Shampoo" collapsed after the party was over. Wife and mistress recognized each other and new choices had to be made.

Experiments with open relationships seemed more common a few years ago: I have seen few people prefer them over any period of time. Penelope was a woman who felt herself very unhappy in a traditional relationship. She had married a rather conventional man, a chiropractor of Hispanic background. He was her third husband, and she liked him in many ways, but their life together was not what she had hoped for. He wanted children, which was medically difficult for her, and she had lost her friends and job when she had relocated for this marriage. In the past, whenever she was uncomfortable with a man, she moved on to someone new, but she found it less easy to do this time. As her marriage slowly dissolved, she found the easiest way to end it was with a somewhat flagrant affair. After that she was really fed up with monogamy.

In group therapy she became quite eloquent: "I'm never going to do it again, never again am I going to be with just one man." She was so convincing that even the most conservative man in the group felt supportive of her decision. I suggested that she join Family Synergy, a support group for people who want to try alternative life-styles; since it seemed inadvisable for her to try this adventure on her own.

There she met a rather prominent and successful architect. Married, he had a large house and offered Penelope a room to rent, and participation as she choose in his extended family. Penelope liked the house, and she was largely left alone. He indicated that she was sexually free both with him, and anyone else, and left her largely alone, which seemed to be her wish.

As she then began to date, she discovered that the more interesting men she met seemed uninterested in her after she told them about her burning disdain for monogamy. Her landlord, Brad, didn't seem to have the problems she had. The end to her free lifestyle came however when Brad had a birthday party. Brad's wife liked the idea of giving him a party, and invited the three or four other women in Brad's life to it. Penelope was just unable to go. It seemed so impossible to her, there was Brad with his family and his loving wife and three other women, while she felt like she had nothing. She had already rejected Brad sexually, but she couldn't acknowledge the fullness of his life at his birthday. Soon he suggested that she move. Her experiment with open relationships was over. She was unable to handle the non-sexual parts of that world: by comparison she had too little.

Disclosure

Why husbands insist on inciting feeling between their wives and mistresses is unclear. Many affairs cause destructive problems only as a result of the stirring up of these jealous feelings; the affair itself is not the problem, but its disclosure is a more serious issue. Often the wife has become a nurturant figure. The husband relates to her not as a companion but as a parent. He wants to run out to play in the world, while needing his wife to remain a secure base for his emotional life. With their increased economic freedom and jealousy of male prerogatives, younger women can do this too, and report having affairs in increasing numbers. (In this vein, we have Balzac's remark in another century: "Marriage is a good place from which to launch an affair.") Often husbands forget that their wives are peers capable of jealousy and relate to them only as symbolic parents who can relieve their guilt. Confession occurs as a way to gain absolution. I've even had patients complain that their spouse is not sufficiently understanding of their problems with their lover! This is a burden too heavy for almost all marriages. Be very certain of your motives before you use your marriage as a place to confess.

While too much exposure and disclosure create

trouble, and suggest that the motive to have the affair included indirect expression of anger towards the spouse, there is another way to manage multiple relations. Including the additional woman, or man, also seems to work, for some of those who attempt it. It didn't work in Penelope's case, because she ended up feeling comparatively short-changed. It worked for **Brad's wife, who appreciated Brad as a good father,** provider, and artistic patron, and who enjoyed her sexual freedom: she wanted less from a new man than Penelope did. Interestingly, the failure of these relationships often occurs in non-sexual matters: one person feels relatively deprived. Although inclusion is not an easy solution, there are a fair number of reports of such relationships continuing for some time. These groupings often require a veto; that is, you can't bring a lover into the relationship who seems inimical to the first relationship, someone who is too threatening or unfriendly to the already present partner.

Not all affairs are adulterous in the psychological sense. Adulterous affairs are those in which the spouse is psychologically present: the adulterous lover is frequently stuggling with resentments over lacks in his marriage. His affair is an imaginary punishment, or revenge to his deficient spouse. A certain number of conscientious and moral people find it difficult to have the affairs that they want unless their spouse does something bad, naughty, intolerable. With this excuse, they now feel free to engage in this "immoral" behavior. These individuals collect injustices the way housewives collect trading stamps. These "brown" injustice stamps are "traded in," or used to justify, affairs. Sometimes needing to justify the affair means the injustices are needed to continue. In this way marital difficulties are maintained.

Other men (and women) don't seem unhappy or angry with their primary relationships. They keep their relationships separate. They don't make love on the marital bed with their lovers. The relationships occupy different spheres, and fill different needs.

How Loss of Trust Destroys Marriages

Recent research shows that about one quarter of American married men and women have had affairs in the first years of marriage. The rate for women now approaches the rate for men. Many marriages seem to have survived affairs. Two issues seem important here. Just as many people seem to feel so guilty about their affair that they need to confess and ask for their spouses absolution, others, equally convinced that they are in mortal danger of being caught and punished, become very deceitful. Afraid that their spouse will punish them, they deceive so thoroughly, that when the affair is disclosed, one way or another (it often happens!) their spouse is furious over the deception. It is this deception which often destroys the marriage.

These trust-breakers are like petty law breakers who kill to preserve their good name; their murders are the awful offense. For the loss of trust in a marriage is in many cases the central issue. When one pretends to be one thing, and turns out to be another, many people can not, do not want to, stay in a relationship with another person. Having sex with another and betraying your husband or wife can be different issues.

Along this line, there are those who chose to have

their affairs with their spouse's best friend. Unwilling to be responsible about their sexual needs, they turn to someone who is handy. Going out and looking for a lover would commit themselves mentally to having an affair, something they internally deny. If they faced this need in themselves more honestly, they would not need to abuse a closeness; they wouldn't simply need to take advantage of what was there. I don't mean to make affairs sound easier than they are. Not everyone accepts their mate having sex outside their principal relationship. Homosexual men living in committed relationships seem most accepting, married women whose husbands are good providers are probably second, although their attitudes are more variable. When someone has a secret affair, the fact that much of their life touches the affair, and is probably not discussed, erodes the marriage further. Are you brave enough to talk about the movie you have seen with your lover, without talking about your lover?

I once briefly treated a prostitute whose problem related to sharing information. She lived with a man, and their understanding was that she only worked as a prostitute for the money, and did not enjoy her work. Most of the time that was true. However, two of her customers had introduced her to the pleasures of suckling at her breasts. She wanted to encourage her lover to do this, but she was afraid that he would get the "wrong idea," and think that she enjoyed her work.

Some people seem to expect to have long physical absences from their mate without their mate becoming sexually active in their absence. I advise my patients that is an unrealistic expectation. This does not mean that every trip means sex! This means that the issue is unpredictable.

Questions To Ask Yourself

Remember that actually writing down your answers or recording them will help you organize your thinking. Discussion of your answers with a friend, afterwards, can be helpful too.

1. It is important to know what the basis is for your affairs, or for your companions'. Is this the way out of an unhappy relationship? Are you looking for a replacement for your spouse?

2. What can you do differently with your outside lover than your primary relationship? Is the sex freer, as is often so? If the answer is " Yes," then ask yourself 2a.

2a. Are you afraid to have a fuller sexual relationship with your partner, or is he or she reticent? (Some patients have reported to me that sex has always been better with their marital partner than any other lover. What they look for is a way out of their boredom in their marriage, and their feeling that they are unduly "hemmed in.")

3. Are you retaliating with an affair to anger over other matters? If the answer to this question is yes, my suggestion is that you comunicate your feelings. The method you have chosen to deal with your anger is dangerous and unlikely to improve things.

11
Confronting Without Destroying

A man I know well has been married five times. I tease him from time to time, telling him he is the truly successful man, with a wife for each season of his life. Like every other American I know who has been married more than once, he, however, sees himself as having failed. What then did he decide to do differently, what did he learn from all his marriages?

He spent a fair amount of time with me between his fourth and fifth marriages. "You've got to learn how they fight, Steve," he would often say to me. "I'm so eager to have that first fight, I can't wait. I just don't know about a woman until I've fought with her," he would add.

I agree. Dealing with, confronting, disagreements and problems is a central part of a long established relationship. Without a workable way to do this, the relationship must fail. It may fail internally, leaving a shell, a marriage in name only. We have all seen those couples in restaurants with nothing to say to each other any more, holding on to each other in polite boredom. When anger and disappointment are held back, it is difficult to open up on other topics. The strain of avoiding unpleasant topics in order to have peace in the relationship kills the natural flow of conversation. Currently, in our culture, such relationships often end in divorce, instead of continuing in disappointment.

Continuing a relationship when there are many painful issues hidden often means that people have to adapt internally in unfortunate ways. Frequently they need to close up and hold back their feelings. Holding back feelings creates a kind of armoring both mentally and physically, that spreads from one unsaid topic to many. Developing the habit of holding in your feelings is often accompanied by a general tenseness and tightness in the muscles that we use to sob, laugh, and love. Furthermore, when there is something on your mind with another person, not saying it may mean that it's hard to talk to them about anything else. Conversation then dries up and withers.

Being polite and respecting others is of course a virtue. Often its practice is more defensive than virtuous; those people who are holding back their negativity imagine that they can improve their relationships by holding back their angry feelings. After all, other people aren't going to change, and they'll just get angry with them. What is forgotten with this argument is what happens to the person who is holding in his angry negative feelings. For many people, this means that they get out of the relationship. Without feeling free to express their negative feelings, they can't stand to be with the person they're angry with.

No two people stay the same. No relationship can last without unforseen problems arising. Unless two people are exactly the same, with exactly the same interests, problems must arise. Differences must develop. Disappointments, unfulfilled wishes are always present. Only a computer feels no passion over these issues, only a computer feels no passion over life.

Once again, I want to emphasize, that when important issues are unexpressed and undealt with in a relationship, it is often hard to talk about anything else. When there are important angry feelings that are held back and unexpressed, it is hard to be loving. Recognizing the importance of self-expression doesn't mean saying everything, every feeling that comes into your head in every situation. A workable rule of thumb is this: Talk about any recurrent feeling or issue that you have with another person.

The realization that some anger is a part of every ongoing relationship is often misapplied. I have known many people who justify their constant fighting and "put-downs" by saying that it is important to express feelings in a relationship. Positive feelings have no chance in such a hostile environment. While unspoken resentment can deaden and poison a relationship, so can constant hurt and the feeling that everything that one does is somehow wrong. We rarely love our critics.

As an atmosphere of hurt, anger, and mistrust envelop a relationship, it may become easier to fight than to love. Sex serves an important tension releasing function. The bound up energy from our responses to the strains and stresses of the day can often be discharged in a loving embrace. Probably, that is the best way. But love-making requires a degree of comfort with another person. Trust and openness make love-making easier. We are vulnerable to our lovers in ways that we are not vulnerable to our enemies, to those we fight with, or laugh at. The tension and bound up feelings that we are left with at the end of the day can also be discharged in laughter, sobbing and rage. Rage too has its orgasm. As love creates love, rage brings forth hurt, anger and rage in another.

Fighting for its own sake, or for tension release, needs to be avoided, or limited in a relationship that you want to last, or be fulfilling. "Necessary" fighting shouldn't be avoided, however.

In the last twenty years psychologists have done a great deal of work understanding how to fight and how to assert oneself. Much has been done developing techniques that allow confrontation while minimizing the creation of hostility in the other. The great value of fighting is that it allows the other people to know what is really important to you, where you are really "at." Some people can never take you seriously without the energy of an angry confrontation. At the same time it is very important to avoid "blaming". Good fights allow you to get your point across, discharge your feelings, and minimize the damage to the other person's self-esteem. Once a clean fight is finished, and feelings have been fully expressed, there is an opening for other feelings.

One technique that helps a lot in confrontations is the use of "I" statements. Often people avoid making "I" statements because it makes them vulnerable. If you say "I want..." or "I hurt when..." then the other person can always say, "So what." That fear, the armoring against disdain and criticism and neglect, makes many people prefer unanswerable generalizations or attacks that lead to counter attacks. Instead of saying "I want..." you may prefer to hide behind, "Any decent person would give me..." Instead of saying "I hurt when..." you may find it easier to say "You are so inconsiderate because you..." Statements like these last will protect your feelings, but are almost guaranteed to lead to further fighting and a lack of understanding. While "I" statements leave you vulnerable, they allow the other person to respond to your needs and feelings without being distracted by an immediate need to defend himself.

Here is an example of what I mean. When your are furious that your hubby doesn't wash the dishes, think of talking like this, like Sally talks to Tom: "I'm absolutely enraged that I can never get you to do the dishes. It's so hard for me to stomach it, frankly, it's hard for me to cook for us. I start cooking and I begin to think, 'That bastard, all I do is cook for him, and he won't even do the damn dishes. Yet I also know that you do a lot of other things. Maybe it's my problem. I don't think you're at fault. You're a good husband in many ways. I don't know what to do about this, except tell you how enraged I get and how difficult this is getting for me."

Notice these important aspects of this example:

1. Strong feeling is communicated

2. What stimulates the strong feeling is revealed. Tom will no longer be mystified any more as to his wife's indifferent cooking. If he is frustrated by her cooking, he has an avenue open for change and improvement.

3. Sally isn't blaming Tom. In other words, Sally isn't saying Tom is morally inferior. Is Tom's dislike of dishwashing any more important in God's scheme of things than Sally's need for help?

Most people feel wrong when a problem is raised, or when you are dissatisfied with something they are doing, even if it is something "right", like loving you a lot. You may not want to be loved at that particular instant, while you are in the middle of cooking for your mother-in-law or watching the last half of the ninth inning in a close baseball game. This almost automatic tendency to feel "wrong" can be partially overcome. It is very important not to contribute to this aspect in a confrontation by saying or implying that something is the matter with the other person.

Once you do that, you shift the discussion to a defensive argument, where the issue becomes the other person's self esteem. He may defensively attack you in some area where he sees you as vulnerable. Fights like this are very common. You talk to him about the dishes and he tells you about the money you're spending. Perhaps you mention his bad breath and the fight continues to escalate. Each of you responds to a felt lowering of self-esteem by saying in some form, "You're another...bad person...even worse."

When you begin to be seen as saying that something is wrong with him, it is easy for him to want to discredit and invalidate you, both because he may want to hurt you back, and because invalidating you may make your criticism of him worthless.

At such moments when you recognize that the person you are confronting feels bad and wants to turn the confrontation to your faults, it is often helpful to say something like the following:

"I'm not trying to say I'm any better than you, we can discuss my failings at some other time. You can make an appointment for a later discussion of your problems with me right now. I do need to discuss this issue, for both our sakes."

There are other ways to communicate the same idea: "I don't want to talk about your problems with me right now, although I'm happy to do so at another time. Right now I want to be sure that you hear me about this problem."

Being Heard

Being heard by the other person is the key to successful confrontations. It is often helpful to ask the other person to repeat back to you what they believe you to have said. How amazed you may be to find out exactly how what you think you said has actually been heard!

In an intimate relationship, it is important to stop confrontations at that point. To get the other person to acknowledge that you are right, or to promise change immediately yourself, is to move away from actually communicating in important areas. Insisting on having an immediate resolution makes winning or losing the fight become the central issue. Once the issue of winning or losing becomes paramount, it becomes distracting. The other person stops responding to the issue at hand, and becomes concerned with a possible loss of self esteem.

Once the other person has heard you, he can respond. Not at that moment, in the midst of anger and hurt, but at another time, when he is interested in making friends, or when the issue you have opened up comes into his consciousness again. If he has any interest in a good relationship with you, he will be at a different place, his actions will be different, because his consciousness of you and your needs are different.

It may seem hard to have a rational confrontation of the kind I am describing. Confrontations often fail when there is a heavy buildup of anger and resentment. When a relationship has many unexpressed problems and grievances, a fight may start, opening a floodgate for accumulated negativity and rage about the relationship. Dealing with so much at once is overwhelming and demoralizing to most people, and makes them doubt the value of the relationship.

Sometimes a pillow fight will help discharge rage, clear your head, and allow you to argue without using your words to wound and hurt. The value of a pillow fight or using Batacas, which are padded clubs, over words, is that rage is muscular, and often needs muscular discharge. In a pillow fight, some of that strong feeling can be discharged. Such contained physical fighting can be a big help because much of our anger may come from old issues that the present conflict has stirred up, or from our general frustration level. All our anger probably doesn't relate to the issue at hand. After the edge is taken from our feelings, our emotional system is freed up and is able to move on to other feelings, other reactions. When we are full of rage a rational discussion is almost impossible and words are used to wound, and to carry part of that anger. Words are remembered, and don't accurately communicate what you want left over from your fight. Words are attended to differently than blows and shouts.

Of course, if you are a man, and want to have a

physical fight with a woman, you need to get her agreement ahead of time to such an activity. One advantage to pillows or Batacas is that they are equalizers. A big person doesn't have a great advantage over a small person in a pillow fight.

Dealing with more than one difficult issue in a relationship is almost impossible. Not long ago a mother who had seen me several years previously with her daughter thanked me in a heartfelt way for help on this point. "My daughter sends her regards," she began. "She's doing quite well in college. I always remember the time we came to see you and you asked me what I wanted different in the relationship. I said 'many things,' and you said, 'that's impossible! Pick one thing. We can only work on one thing at a time'. So I picked dangerous and drunken driving with her friends. She's alive now and doing quite well."

When one faces an accumulation of problems in a relationship it is easy to want to "dump" them all on the head of the other. That's only worth doing when you're absolutely certain you don't want the relationship to continue. Then a good dump session is a fine way to say good-by and burn your bridges to the past.

It is a common recognition that it's better to deal with problems before they get to that point. One way to do that is to alert the other person to what you are uncomfortable about with a simple remark, made in passing. Remarks like these:

"Doing the dishes this often bothers me."
"I miss having dinner together more often."
"I'm beginning to have the sense that our sex life isn't what it once was, and that bothers me."

This last remark is best not made in during love-making. Remarks made more or less in passing don't really require responses. They have a double value: they prevent the build-up of unexpressed feeling and they alert the other person to what is on your mind. When you find that an issue persists in being a problem, you can then call for a dialogue.

It is worthwhile to make an appointment for an important confrontation. Dialogues are not mono-logues, the other person must be open to hear you. He has a right to a time that is suitable for him. After all, he may be facing stress at work, or someplace else, and not truly be open to hear you at this time.

When you do begin your confrontation, remember, talk about your feelings honestly, reveal their importance to you, and don't blame. Your feelings probably reflect many things about your life. The needs you have will be hopefully filled by your partner and lover. Your need doesn't necessarily mean he is bad or deficient. He may not have known your needs, in their intensity, or they may have changed.

The purpose of confronting is to make your life different. That is not the same as "getting something off your chest." It is important to express yourself, and it gives many people great pleasure to freely express themselves. One of the sweetest pleasures I know comes from fully disclosing oneself, and discovering that one is still loved and accepted.

The unquestioned value of self-expression has lead to a certain confusion in some. Self-expression is not man's only value. Undoubtedly it's better in most situations to fight and be openly unpleasant than to be a martyr. Certainly blocked feeling has a great deal to do with physical illness. It is usually helpful for another person to know what your attitudes and feelings are.

But a life of being angry should not be man's goal. It is better to change your life so that you don't need to be always angry. That angry energy needs to be put back into your relationships in a useful way. Energy ought to be used to transform the relationship into one where you're not always angry.

We have in our culture a new and widespread theory of emotions, which I call the "toilet-bowl theory of feeling": feelings are something to be "gotten rid of", expressed—and then forgotten. Like shit, we get rid of it, we express it, and then we flush the toilet, forgetting the cause and basis of our feelings. Our feelings need to be attended to as valuable guides to the direction of our life. Our anger says something valuable about our values and their intensity, both to others and ourselves.

Questions To Ask Yourself

Remember that writing down your answers will help you to think more clearly, and be honest with yourself. Discussing your written answers with someone who knows you will help you know yourself better.

1. Are you willing to tell people what you are angry about? When you do, is it your habit to tell the other person what is the matter with them, and therefore lower them, or do you simply deal with it as an annoying or infuriating difference?

12
Endings

An ex-partner had lunch with me as our partner-ship ended and said "We'll get together." I've not seen him since. We both feel lucky.

A patient ended her marriage in a stormy way when she was fairly young. I was her husband's therapist through the divorce. First he went off for a summer institute and had an affair. His wife got mad and sent him packing. She had an affair. Jerry got mad. Susie got pregnant. He met a new woman whom he later married and divorced. Susie divorced him. Jerry moved away. Susie came to see me as a patient for a while.

"Am I glad to be done with him," she said. Susie said that for at least a year, then the tears came. More than once, in group therapy she would have to leave to cry: deep racking sobs for hours. Her mourning lasted several years. Only when she had completed it could she find a new man and remarry.

Cam was married for twenty-five years and his kids were grown. His somewhat emotional wife drank too much. Quiet and long-suffering he said little. He spent two years in a therapy designed to help him express his feelings. He complained of no results. Cam and Mary went to friends for dinner. "You really are a good cook," Cam said to his hostess at the dinner party.

"You never say that to me," Mary said. Cam said nothing. At least he had expressed himself, although not favorably as far as Mary was concerned.

"I can't live this way any more," Mary said. "Let's get a divorce." They did, although they continued to have dinner together for many years, every other week.

A rather brilliant, anxious, and abrasive student came to see me about problems with his faculty in a natural science department. His relationships improved with his teachers. He met a young girl and married. Poor, he lived with her and her parents. He was accepted in graduate school and they moved away.

He was happy. His wife, Penny, took a few courses too. One of them was in women's studies. She looked at their relationship somewhat differently after the course. They didn't fight, however. One weekend he went away hunting with some friends.

"Penny seemed fine when I left," Dave said. "When I got home, she had left me a note saying she didn't want to live with me any more, I was too much of a male chauvinist." She refused to see him again. They divorced in the minimum time allowed by law.

As I reflect on these endings, I become aware of how little effective communication there is in relationships that end. People change and relationships change. Those people who confront well and communicate fully manage to stay in relationships longer. As people's feelings, attitudes, and needs change, their partners and lovers need to hear the changes, so that they may change also.

Communicating Avoids Ending

As I have said here earlier, a willingness to communicate problems is really what defines a committed relationship. The key in that sort of communication is getting heard. Hopefully, communicating about our problems will lead the other to change, if not, we at least have the momentary relief of self-expression. When change doesn't come about, we need to let the other person know how important this issue is to us; important enough perhaps to end the relationship as it is.

Without letting the other person know that you may end the relationship over your differences, he may not realize the importance you place on the problem. It is often difficult to communicate this without sounding like you are giving an ultimatum: Change immediately, this is your last chance. While ultimatums are undesirable, it is still necessary to let the other person know the depth of your feeling, and the likely outcome. One way to do this is to say something like the following: "You probably ought to know that I think of leaving over this problem. I don't know if I'll do it, but I do think of it, and that is quite unusual for me."

Those who follow this procedure rarely seem to end their relationships. Since their whole stance is a relational one, I can see why that is true. My preference is to only threaten the end of a relationship very sparingly. It is not easy to "end" a relationship since once we know another person, it is always possible and frequently easy to start anew. Old relationships that have ended are always in some form of abeyance, "on hold." Some relationships are almost impossible to end, whatever words are said, like that of a delinquent child and his parent.

Politicians seem to understand this point best of all, and for this reason are frequently accused of shallow and treacherous relationships. Julius Caesar, master political strategist of all time, was known for the quick and generous acceptance he gave to his former enemies. All he required was a letter, and he would generously repair the relationship, frequently with a dinner.

Transforming Instead of Ending

I think it is a better proceedure to transform a relationship than to end it. What good remains between the two of you may be preserved, to your mutual benefit.

Businesses recognize this when they lose a very important employee and make him into a consultant. The business has the benefit of his knowledge. The employee has some portion of his salary, and the chance to use that part of himself developed in his old job. Sometimes he will even keep his office at a reduced level.

To do this in a personal relationship a period of preparation may be necessary, when one partner indicates that a certain part of a relationship may end, weakening, thinning the relationship as a whole. At the same time it is important to emphasize that you are not ending the relationship totally, and you want to stay on good terms with your friend. You still want to keep those parts of your relationship that seem viable, whatever they may be. You will have to stay steadfast to avoid his counter-rejection and a further decrement in the relationship. You may want to drop activities ranging from having sex, cooking dinner, going to the movies together, seeing your spouse's friends, or anything not mutually agreeable.

A proper transformation of a relationship from close to distant, or to some intermediate point, doesn't have to involve a lot of blaming and fighting. Decreasing a relationship does require a recognition of separateness. We must see the other as another, with interests and needs unlike ours. Additionally, there are special problems and anxieties that plague relationships in decline that require understanding and self-discipline.

When people change, their needs change and their relationships may no longer fulfill their best interests. The person who is left must face his life without this significant other. He faces a loss while the person leaving goes to a new life, or at least a potential future of his own choice. The person who is left automatically feels diminished, his life is smaller. The person leaving sees in his imagination a new and better life. Often, of course, new hopes and ventures fail, and life turns out exactly the opposite. Many a complaining spouse has discovered that his mate has taken all his complaints to heart, and changed radically with another person.

When we begin a relationship, finding some companion to be with in our life, we are generous and giving, expecting little or nothing in return. Under these circumstances, our gifts of love and friendship bring forth gifts from the other, and we are surprised to discover a similar liking and generosity. Soon this process accelerates, like generates like, affection creates affection, love causes love, or finds it, since these matters are often reciprocal.

Relationships go downhill in a similar way. First there is a withdrawal, and then we find that the other is not there when we expected, in the way we expected and knew from the past. We forget our own withdrawal and its causes, and see the other as leaving us. Rejection breeds counter rejection. Few people like to be left, and as a relationship diminishes, each person protects himself. It is as difficult to stop this process as it is to stop two people from falling in love.

The danger in shifting a relationship to a less intensive mode is that it may create a dissolution beyond what is wanted or needed. Couples with children, who are truly bound together for a long time, often get to this place. When relationships come to an end there are many difficult issues. In marriage there is a universal feeling of failure. I have seen no exception to this, no matter how unconventional or independent the person. The strong concern over failure often leads to blaming and attacks on the other. Generally there is a great deal of hurt, a strong desire to retaliate, a denial of need for the other person, as well as a desire to get on with one's life. Managing feelings of hurt, failure, and rejection are the keys to dissolving and changing relationships.

Not only is it necessary to manage one's own feelings in these matters, but it is very important to tolerate the other person's adjustment to the break, in hopes of not driving the relationship further into the ground than meets everyone's best interests.

Frequently I hear people say things like "Time heals all wounds," or "Give things time." Actually time does nothing, events are curative, time has no properties. We can see this in the physical world clearly. Iron rusts, but in air or water, not in deep space. It will rust in time, but only if there is oxygen to oxidize it. Similarly with the hard feelings over breakups. Anger will fade, if the angry person constructs a new life for himself, learns new things about life, and notices that you don't have it much better without him. Perhaps he has early pleasant memories that remain to overshadow the bitter, later ones. Other events may intervene to change angry feelings, or any feelings. But if nothing *happens* to fill and alter feelings, then these painful old feelings will remain.

Couples who break up and wish to keep their relationship from totally dissolving have had some success by scheduling regular and not too frequent meetings, say twice a month for dinner. At such time, unresolved feelings and misunderstandings can be aired, and whatever is salvageable in the relationship may be maintained. There is a frequent phenomeneon of relationships continuing and improving after divorce. Part of this has to do with a shift in futurity: when people no longer feel stuck with each other forever they often treat each other somewhat differently. No longer is it necessary to drive the other away to establish freedom for oneself. Out there alone many people discover that their former spouse has many desirable characteristics not easily discovered in others.

Loss generates grief and opportunity, pain and joy. Many people feel that one set of feelings is OK to have and not the other. Actually our feelings fluctuate as we are alternately aware of the advantages and disadvantages of our loss. A relationship determines who we are;

when we are out of it we have the opportunity to be someone else with others. We have the opportunity and difficulty of organizing our lives differently.

Women frequently report not being able to be themselves in a committed relationship. In a relationship they need to totally orient themself to the man in their life. A woman like this had come to see me for a minor pain in her side. There was no apparent physical cause and she noticed that the pain went away when she took a mild tranquilizer. She reported one other "minor" symptom that marred her marriage of twenty-five years: occasionally she would imagine taking a knife and plunging it in her husband's back. It was she who said to me, as she ended her stifling and disappointing marriage, the unusual and interesting phrase: "The happiest day in a woman's life is the day of her first divorce."

13
Intimacy

Our need for intimacy is clear in infancy. Infants raised without holding, stroking, and attention lose their interest in life and the things about them, shrink away, give up and even die. Without physical closeness and caring, life is not worth living, to a pre-verbal infant. As we grow older and words and ideas become more important, we need words. A "hello" to an adult is like a pat on the back, or a hug, is to a child.

Children without too many conflicts need someone to "tell their day to", that is part of intimacy. They still need the physical contact of earlier times, although that often diminishes for a while. Adult intimacy has special characteristics both verbally and physically. The physical intimacy of sex is only a partial solution for many people. Adults, too, benefit from sharing, although many have become so armored, resigned, and despairing of human contact that they can go on for years without any apparent close or private relationships. Many adults develop a system of minimal or even partial sharing that apparently suffices to maintain their lives, until they begin an affair with someone who they are willing to be open with. Someone who can hear their secret hopes and fears.

When we no longer feel heard by our partner in important ways, sexual intimacy becomes boring and a chore. Conversely, psychotherapists, those hearers of secrets, become the object of desire. For intimacy spreads back and forth from one area to another, verbal to physical, physical to verbal. Often the most tight lipped men can reveal themselves a bit after a sexual encounter, a fact perennially useful to secret intelligence services.

The famous psychiatrist Eric Berne reportedly claimed we were lucky to have a total of five minutes of game-free intimacy in our life. Berne saw most human activities as manipulations, struggles for covert gains, repititions of painful early life experiences that were played out in hidden ways. Ways that the other participants in our lives were often unaware of. We wrote scripts for our lives that only were meaningful to us, the others who we inveigled into our games found themselves pushed around for our hidden needs. He was suspicious too of much of what passed for feeling in our culture, seeing much dramatization or use of apparent feeling as another way to have a desired impact on another person. Like most psychoanalytically trained doctors, he didn't see such maneuvers as generally conscious. Such games and maneuvers seem the antithesis of intimacy, which for him and others is game-free, child-like, a free and playful exchange.

I find this chapter more difficult to write than any other. The very spontaneous, child-like aspects of intimacy are alien to my goal directed activity of writing sensibly. This chapter can only hint, it speaks of the hard to describe, the ineffable. Perhaps a poem, or a prayer would be better.

The dictionary describes intimacy as "...a close personal relationship especially marked by affection or love...marked by breadth of knowledge or broadness of understanding...a complete intermixture, compounding or interweaving..." I am more optimistic than Berne, I think it is possible to do much better, although I recognize that most people, most of the time, are trying to get "more" in some way or other, and that this goal-oriented characteristic stands in the way of the deepest intimacies.

Intimacy in Psychotherapy

The need for various kinds of intimacy is not talked about much, and is part of what psychotherapy is about. Part of the reason that some psychotherapeutic relationships continue for long periods of time, is the absence of truly intimate friendships in the ordinary life of the patient. Some people who have noted the part that filling intimacy needs plays in the continuation of psychotherapy have talked about therapy as the purchase of friendship, a kind of verbal prostitution, rising as our culture creates more loneliness and isolation.

Much of the structure of psychotherapy is designed to provide a setting that allows patients to have intimacy. By the fact that the typical therapist plays no active part in his patient's life, while simultaneously being well paid for his time, he is disposed to be open and non-critical of his patient's secrets. The patient is encouraged to tell all. Once the patients secrets are disclosed, the therapist neither discloses or exploits them, an attitude we wish for from our friends.

Therapists however are ethically, even legally, required to be this way. The patient at least has someone to be intimate with, although this intimacy is principally one way. Much of the pleasure of psychotherapy for us who practice it comes from the pleasure of experiencing other people as they truly are.

To some extent, our patients try the same games with us as they try with other people; they look for our approval, try to make us into fools, or cheats, or gods, depending on how they need to see others. If the therapist is honest, patient, competent, and lucky enough to work with someone he can understand, these maneuvers can end, at least in that special situation. Therapists, then by their profession, are specially suited to understand intimacy, and one of the oldest methods of psychotherapy, free association, is one of the best methods to produce it.

Intimacy with Friends

Intimacy between two people can be understood as a special two way version of the method of free association: two people, speaking freely whatever comes to mind, without holding back, without considering the effects of their remarks on the other. That other, the thou, is free to do the same thing. Intimacy is not limited to words only; from them can come play of various kinds, and sexual explorations and pleasures.

Despite the fact that I am more optimistic than Berne, the examples that spring to my mind are few. I think of myself with my friend Gary, walking along the Pacific Ocean one evening. We've known each other well, we come from similar environments, and we've given up on making something special of our friendship. Working together leads to no community of interests, we've tried that. Neither of us are homosexual, we have no compelling need for each other in that way. Sex doesn't spring to mind when we are together. What is left is friendship, sharing. After we've shared our worst worries, we talk about whatever occurs: he speaks, I speak in response. I don't think much about what I am going to say, if I do at all. I feel as free as I am to speak to myself...almost. Gary and I have no ax to grind with each other. We see little advantage in our friendship except what we're doing with each other at the moment.

In many ways intimacy is easier in a relationship where nothing is wanted. The desire to more than simply "be" with another person stimulates our need to grasp, pressure, manipulate, lie, and dissimulate. Letting things occur naturally, not trying to push the river, going with the flow, these are all phrases that have been used to encourage a kind of behavior that is a pre-requisite for intimacy. Importance and naturalness do not go hand in hand. A patient of mine described to me her first date with a man she was very interested in. They worked together in separate divisions of a large firm. She had been sociable towards him, finally he asked her for lunch. "Oh what a disaster," she said to me.

"Didn't he like you?" I asked naively.

"Well, I hardly said a word. I couldn't even swallow my food. He must know I'm crazy about him. He probably thinks I'm a nerd."

"Perhaps he thinks you're quiet," I said, hopefully.

"No. He knows I'm not quiet. Now he knows how

much I like him and he hasn't even asked me out again. I'm so embarrassed, I never want to see him again."

Sex with inappropriate people, one night stands, even prostitutes, can often be easier than that tense lunch. For in those inappropriate relationships there is no need to do anything special, to succeed , to win someone in love, to be affirmed. What happens, happens. In sex, where spontaneity and naturalness is almost a physiological necessity, concern with the other person's opinion has a destructive effect. Not only can this concern make sexual activity awkward and mechanical, but concern with the other's good opinion can make experimentation difficult.

When we are concerned with the opinion of an important other, it certainly is difficult to tell them our secret sexual fantasies. Thus our sexual life limits itself. When we are protective of our partner's feelings, and see them as weak, in need of our protection, it is hard to tell them how dissatisfied we are sexually.

In Love and Marriage

Men are seemingly less easy about intimacy, especially with their wives, who seem to long for it, in most middle class marriages. Often I hear the complaint from wives that their husbands share little. In these cases I recommend that the husband simply follow the old psycho-analytic rule of free association...or as close to it as he can get with someone who is important to him...and share his private thoughts. This is a simple solution; it works, and it's a scary one, for that very reason.

Marriages suffer by comparison to affairs because the intimacy in marriages is less. The lover often knows about the mate, and has therefore a freer relationship with her friend than the spouse does. Also, a new relationship with two roughly comparable people is easier. This ease relates to subjects that can no longer be discussed: dead ends and cul-de-sacs. There are other advantages to newness, certain intimacies are easier with a fresh person who has not dismissed your arguments, and who doesn't have certain known sensitivities and blind spots that must constantly be skirted.

Recognizing that we tend to clam up when someone is important to us must make the issue of love and marriage seem almost hopeless to some. Consciousness of the contradictory and opposing forces in relationships, however, puts us in a better position to resolve them. A perfectly intimate relationship that lasts forever requires a special kind of saint: someone perfectly free to act as he wishes, and take whatever painful consequences arise. Lesser mortals can decide to share intimacies to a greater degree than they have before, knowing that their choice will keep their relationship more alive.

14
Money and Equality

Money heavily influences the division of labor in a relationship, the distribution of prestige; it is a token of affection, a necessary evil, a poor substitute for love, a way to buy love.

Money is a symbol whose possession can symbolize many things we want: importance, power, fame, love, usefulness. It can also be used to buy things we need or think we will enjoy.

Benjamin Franklin said, "A man has three friends, an old dog, an old wife, and ready money."

Some say "Everyone has a price," but we don't usually pay for favors in an intimate relationship, in fact, that is typically the mark of a business arrangement instead of an intimate relationship: friendship, love, or marriage. We don't pay our intimates for favors. In these close relationships, the rule is some form of sharing. Furthermore, in an intimate relationship we can't compute every exchange of favors too precisely without losing closeness, spontaneity , and intimacy. Even if we wished to we would find the difficulties enormous, since there is no readily available, impersonal, pricing mechanism.

Division of labor issues are part of any small intimate group of equals. To some degree we expect those who share in the benefits equally to work equally, and vice versa. In various cultures we see many different ways of dividing up life's work between men and women, depending on the culture's history, technical resources, accidents, myths and realities about the nature of men and women.

Some kind of typical, usual sexual division of labor is almost universal in human culture until now. A number of cultures reverse our particular distribution of sex roles, giving dominating and prestigious roles to women. In others there are varying degrees of freedom from the necessity of choosing a typical man's or woman's role. All societies recognize that some individuals refuse to fit into sex-role typing.

Before World War I the family model in our largely agricultural society required a busy woman running the home, washing the clothes, making the meals, taking care of the many children. She tended to work harder often than her husband, who worked more often in the fields, perhaps in a factory. There too he needed a homemaker to take care of his larger structure of care: cooking, washing, care during illness. With the introduction of labor-saving devices at home, the married woman's necessary work to keep a household running became less and less. With improved birth-control methods easily available, family size began to shrink and come under conscious control. Under the emergency conditions of World War II suddenly these economically superfluous women were called upon to work in factories. They did so quite well. Slowly, in the post-war period the culture began to adapt to the use of women in the general labor market. Now we are in the middle of a transition period where the economic division of labor between men and women is unclear, and the cultural effects and values are not yet stabilized. Many different systems co-exist in our culture, and unless there are clear understandings, relationships get into severe trouble.

Adapting to the New Economy

It is important to recognize an underlying principle despite the many different financial arrangements possible in the United States. Financial equality can only exist when there is some basic equality in useful work effort.

Eating out, paying for a date, is often a way that women and men signal the kinds of economic arrangements they expect in a more committed relationship. Some men insist on paying the whole check. It is of course clear that they are signalling their intention to be providers, if they actually commit themselves to marriage, or a similarly financially responsible relationship. Some women offer to pick up the check, less common now than ten years ago. More often women will offer to pay the tip. That's a very unclear message for most men. Is the woman saying she wants symbolic financial equality, or is momentarily short of cash, can't stand to receive a gift, or wants to be treated like a financial equal without making an equal contribution?

Along this line, a patient of mine reported the

following incident. He had taken his date to a rather expensive dinner, after which she offered to pay the tip. He wanted more reciprocity than that, and declined. On their second date Julia offered to pay for the parking. Again he declined, saying, "If you want to do something, you can get dessert after dinner, maybe at the Cafe Casino." After dinner, Julia decided that the Cafe Casino had something the matter with it, evidently the desserts were too expensive. She suggested another place. Tom and Julia went there. It was crowded and dirty. He suggested going back to the Cafe Casino. There, Tom ended paying for dessert. Such incidents are good opportunities for clarifying conversations.

Both men and women are having problems adapting to the current scene where approximately half of married women work. This proportion is even higher in the more recently married. At the same time that women have entered the cash for services part of the economy in large numbers, their wages are very variable. Sometimes they earn as much as their fellow male workers, usually somewhat less, either because they are working in lower paid occupations, some remnants of sex discriminaton, or because they are somewhat irregular as workers, and their earnings suffer as a consequence. The extreme variability in women's economic position currently makes it difficult for new cultural rules to develop.

The partner who has more money in an ongoing relationship has more influence on many topics. Recent survey data indicates that in all kinds of intimate relationships, with the exception of lesbian pairs, the larger economic provider has more influence. How money is spent in vacations, the use of disposable income generally, is heavily influenced by who makes more. The acceptance by married women of their husband's sexual activity outside of marriage seems linked, for traditional women, to their financial dependence on men. Lesbian couples however, perhaps as a rebellion against being under men's economic thumb, are quite heavily focused on equality.

Many men are very attached to the traditional provider role. For centuries it has given men a great deal of social power, deferential treatment at home, and sexual compliance, if not sexual love. Currently, however, the average business executive may find himself treated deferentially at the office, but harried, belittled, and ignored at home, except when his money is wanted. Many men feel like nothing outside of their role as economic provider. No wonder they have a hard time giving it up. Other women complain of their husband's economic ineffectiveness , masking their resentment over not being taken care of as they had imagined, growing up in another time, planning a different future.

Other men rebel, they are afraid of the apparent burden of taking care of a woman and HER children. In today's economic culture, it is relatively easy for a single person to manage to eat well, get his clothes cleaned, get taken care of when he is sick, live in a clean place, without giving up his freedom to relate sexually to whomever he wishes for as long as he wishes. Many men who see marriage in its traditional economic organization put off marriage until they feel economically secure. Unwilling to make a stable connection of any other kind, they feel inadequate to carry out their quasi-traditional dream. In one way they are right, for in today's economic world, few men can easily generate by themselves the cash income required for a family. As the culture changes, wages are beginning to reflect the expectation that there will be two major wage earners in a family. Thus while many men put off marriage until they feel economically secure, the economic reality is that they will not get to be secure economically until they team up with a female wage-earner.

Many women are so concerned about keeping from being "exploited" that the economic arrangements they are wanting to make will get no takers from a self respecting man. Here as elsewhere, self-knowledge is crucial. Sally, a young mental health worker, kept telling me how badly she wanted to be married. Her reasons were unclear: her father was brilliant and eccentric with a rather formal marriage. Mother had her philanthropic activities while father had his profession, casual women, and drinking. Occasionally her brother would get a call during the early morning hours from their father asking to be taken home from some hotel where he had gotten stranded with a prostitute.

Sally didn't want to be stuck in a bad marriage. She was sure of that. She made that clear to the men she dated. Most important she wanted children. And if the marriage didn't work, she would take the children and divorce, unlike her mother. When she did marry and have children, her husband could expect to share every household and child rearing task equally. If the relationship didn't work she fully expected to end the marriage and keep the children. He would naturally pay child support.

An equitable arrangement, you may be thinking? She could find no man willing to take it. For the man was undertaking a long term financial and personal obligation to provide for children; children she fully expected to stay with her, no matter what happened to the marriage. Unless he was as keen as she to have children, while simultaneously caring little about whether he lived with them, he would realize that this arrangement was not in his interests.

Sally, like many contemporary women, knew that a traditional marriage had been a rip-off for her mother and many in that previous generation. Unfortunately, like many of her sisters, she believed that the solution was to be as miserable and exploitive to men in turn as they had been to women. She needs to recognize that the men she meets were not the ones who constructed those oppressive relationships she observed as a child. Further, women colluded with men, it was the system, more than particular individuals, that was oppressive.

Pooling Money

Often more traditional couples have a difficult time respecting their separate economic needs. Total financial merging becomes a tool in pretending that there is a greater commonality and personal fusion than actually exists. In these relationships individuality is seen as threatening.

I worked with a young woman for many months who had no money of her own. She accounted to her husband for every dime she spent. Poor, they shopped together. Their marriage was much improved when she was given an allowance of ten dollars weekly to dispose of as she needed to. At first, the separateness that the ten dollars implied was too much for their fused relationship. Her husband was quite suspicious of her need for money, and felt somewhat abandoned by her. With time, he could see her treatment of him improve, and he became more accepting.

At the other end of the economic scale a couple that led quite separate lives, with separate incomes, and business activities insisted on keeping a single joint account. Joanne was a sharp businesswoman who extended her credit to its limit. Her conservative husband wanted to keep his creditors less agitated. Joanne would consistently overdraw their joint account, as she dealt with a succession of crises. Nonetheless, he refused to have a separate bank account. That meant to him a further separateness in their lives already too disjoined. This symbolic joint account was a source of constant argument between them.

Both men and women are struggling to free themselves of a world view based on the man being the sole cash provider. Many who give lip service to accepting our changed economic circumstances have not faced how deeply rooted their attitudes over money and work are. There are still numbers of women who see their work as somehow temporary, not serious, any income is for some temporary project, or theirs alone. Their husband's earnings of course belong to both of them. Stuck with the idea that being a provider is their principal claim to importance in a relationship, their husband's greet their wives' re-entry into the job market with the fear of losing them. For if their women can take care of themselves in the big world, they may not need a husband. These attitudes, like the partially economic basis of marriage itself, are deeply rooted, and will not evaporate overnight. In these situations men need a fair amount of explicit reassurance, somewhat hard to give while they are protesting that they don't need it. Women, on the other hand, require trust as they struggle to adapt to the changed economy and their need for a less housebound life.

The payoff in a marriage is quite substantial for resolving these problems. Many of the families that are functioning well economically these days are those where both man and wife have significant careers and corresponding incomes. In dealing with this area it is helpful to share with your other, your own early learnings in this area. What did your parents do? Watching them, how did you feel about their economic arrangement? Is this what you expected when you grew up? Did you, as a woman, choose to underdevelop your career because you always secretly expected some man to take care of you? How do you feel now about that decision? Did you, as a man, focus all your energy on work activities, expecting to have a loving and fully attentive woman as your reward?

15
Love

Leaving love until this late may seem strange, in a book on loving relationships. The word is used in so many different, at times contradictory ways, that I wished to wait until I had clarified some of the core issues before I tackled this confusing word. Often "love" refers to sexual desire, more often it refers to need. Its use is avoided by authentic people, and cold ones; while hot-blooded people use it almost as freely as the hypocrites. Certainly it is a confusing term. There is a ritual where one person will say, "I love you," expecting his partner to say, "I love you," in return. This is a statement of mutual need, not an authentic statement of affection or sympathy or desire.

The unabridged Oxford dictionary has four pages of definition of the word: "...a feeling of natural attraction and sympathy manifesting itself in a feeling of solicitude for the welfare and delight in the presence... warm affection...strong devotion or predilection to something, ...sexual affection...doing something without stakes, for play or affection... to entertain a great affection or regard, a passionate attachment to a person of the opposite sex...to be strongly attached or unwilling to part with or perish...to have a strong liking or addiction for...to have great pleasure in doing something...to praise, flatter..."

Several ideas underlie these definitions. Important to our understanding of relationships are three: delight, value, and attachment. The revolution in the Western world away from arranged marriages had to do with the first issue. Relationships without pleasure and delight in the other are a strain and a bore.

Caring vs Attachment

Often love problems arise when there is a conflict between love meaning "attachment" and love meaning "caring". Letting go of someone whose closeness and companionship we delight in or need may be called for. Their best interests may require separation from us, and they may or may not recognize this. Sometimes we need to let our dependents, our children, be taken care of by others, but they may not understand our illness, our incapacity. More commonly, as children become young adults, they often need to leave us. We cannot be the whole world for them. Perhaps we will see them again, more or less frequently, perhaps not. Our caring for them forces on us the recognition that they will complete their development better in other company, other activities.

Between adult lovers it often occurs that interests don't coincide. We may not be in a position to offer our loved one what he truly needs. He may recognize that his interests require leaving, but we still feel attached and don't want to lose him. More confusing still is the situation when someone thinks he can do better with another person, or in another situation. We may think he's wrong. What then do we do? Ought we leave the relationship in abeyance, and still see him while he explores other relationships, other settings? Perhaps this will simply make us a launching pad while he seeks another lover. We support him as he develops a new relationship, while we suffer his foolish abandonment. On the other hand, why should he bother to come back to us if we weren't really his friend, and only cared about him when he was attached to us?

Without real love, who wants a close relationship? That was the message of that nineteenth century revolution in matters of love, celebrated in many operas and older novels. To my Aunt Gertie's remark that it is as easy to fall in love with a rich person as a poor one there is the proverbial reply, "He who marries for money, earns it." Delight and pleasure in the other makes what would otherwise be a difficult sacrifice, an easy passage for the sake of being together.

It is hard to be in a close relationship when one has little happy regard for people. When one is unhappy and bitter, and sees others as miserable creatures, the pleasant basis of being together seems alien. When the bitterness is not too overwhelming, it may be overcome by a happy and loving relationship. More often the difficulties in loving a bitter person will collapse the relationship. Occasionally people still try to establish close relationships without genuine caring for the other person. These relationships are essentially hopeless over the long term. It is true that in other cultures love might develop over the course of the relationship, since the betrothed were essentially strangers to each other. Sexual intimacy, the experience of a shared life struggle, the pleasures of children, and pressures from society have created love among many relative strangers. In our freer culture, companionship and mutual knowledge exists before marriage. A sexual relationship is usually possible if at least one person wants it badly, the other is not abnormal and marriage is likely. In our world, an engagement or a long relationship where strong loving feelings do not develop and remain forewarns of a dead and uninteresting marriage.

I recall once dining alone in a plush resort hotel. A woman was dining alone nearby and we ended up having dessert together. She seemed very friendly and open despite her sad expression. Her story was interesting. It was her honeymoon, and her husband was sick in their room. She had lived abroad for five years, and reaching the age of thirty-one years, she decided to marry a home town boy she had known for years. She returned home, married him, and was now sitting unhappily married, talking to her first new friend on her honeymoon. Given her lack of genuine interest in her husband, she would probably need many new friends over the course of her marriage.

In our world, relatively few people attempt marriage when there is little love. More often there is love at the beginning of a relationship, commitment grows, living together and marriage ensue, and love vanishes. The relationship remains, and the former lovers stay together for a short or long period, too stunned by the disappearance of their love for each other to know what to do.

How Love Destroys Itself

In our current culture, contrasted with a century and more ago for the majority of people, love is celebrated and valued. Love's problems come more often from love's initial presence, not its absence. Central to understanding love is understanding the effects on a person when he becomes connected to something he values highly. For underlying all forms of love is a tremendous valuation of the other. Perhaps not everything valued is loved, but everything loved is valued highly. We can and do react differently to the presence of someone or something that we value enormously depending on our ability or intention to attach ourselves to the valued person, or object.

Valuing the other, a prerequisite for a decent relationship, creates its own problems. We can value someone or something and not feel any attachment. We do this in a museum, or a movie theatre, or at the beach or airport when a beautiful stranger passes us. We can admire a movie star, and it causes us no more problem than a moments jealousy from our date. When we really value, "love", our date in an attached way, our troubles have begun. We start our relationships because we want companionship, perhaps we need more than a body next to us. We need someone to relate to. Once we have discovered how wonderful it is to have this fantastic lover close to us, we become afraid. We keep our thoughts secret in fear of losing her.

Paradoxically, the end of love starts from its intensity. As I said earlier, people need a relationship, because they don't want to be alone, because they need more than sex from the opposite sex. Once they have a relationship, once they have found the other they have searched for, they become frightened. Now, the relationship is too valuable to use. We are careful to avoid giving offense to our partner, telling them things they don't want to hear, acting as we need to act, more or less openly. So the relationship dies. First it becomes something to use in the future, in an emergency, when we really need it. Then the relationship becomes just a symbol of itself, a potential. Thus "All men kill the thing they love..." To keep a relationship, one must be brave enough to use it.

Love vs The World

When great valuing of the other leads to great need for them, we are in trouble. A character in one of the earliest English writings we have remarks, "True love is an absolute disaster." So it may be, making us wish to abandon everything else we have valued in our life. A more cynical modern defiantly declares, "Love, Bardamu, is a puppy dog's chance at the infinite, and personally I'm too proud."

This statement too deserves inspection. Often in love we are acting as if we were once again two years old, completely dependent on our mothers for survival, and deriving all that is good from being in her arms. In love, we give up the world for the arms of our beloved. At two years of age, our mother was the center of our life. She was the source of our food, provider of our play, our protector. She also had the uncanny ability to know our needs without our needing to speak. An ability we often vainly look for in later lovers.

An attachment to a mother figure, who may be a father, or a nurse, seems to be part of our biological inheritance. Her loss apparently causes the most severe damage between the age of eighteen months and three years, but is never easy. Those adults who long most painfully for a close love relationship often suffered early abandonment. Many times that abandonment has led to numbness about their neediness. However, even in their case, an intense need for the exclusive caring love of another often lies beneath their calloused self presentation. Others have never physically lost their caring parent, but they have never had a good one. As one patient said, "Seeing other kids with nice parents was like being in a candy store with no money." Like many others, she brought to her adult love relationships the residues of her early need for a good attachment figure.

Adult pleasure is another matter, the pleasure of being in the world creeps up to compete with our infantile love pleasures, and a love affair that stays closed to the outside world, usually begins to pall. For a brief while, being in love is like being on an island, and our beloved is sufficient. Later, the world calls. We want more than this closeness, this skin contact, this understanding.

The call to be in the world is love's great competitor. Handling this other need is the chief problem in the best of matches. Recognizing it as not a diminution of the loved person helps somewhat. No single person can expect to compete with the whole world. Tolstoy's famous novel *Anna Karenina* is as good a representation of this problem as we usually see. Here Anna runs off and away from her boring marriage to be with a dashing cavalry officer. The year they have together begins delightfully, but slowly Vronsky begins to long for his life in the army, in society. He returns to Russia. Anna, with less options, throws herself on the train tracks.

This opposition between the call of love and the call of society is a common theme of romantic literature at the end of the nineteenth century. The opera *Madame Butterfly* can be considered to deal really with the same issue. Men, who at that time had more options, abandoned their most delightful loves for the work of society and the company of less satisfying women.

In this time, in the United States in the last quarter of the twentieth century, we are more optimistic. We hope to have great love and fulfilling work at the same time. In a way this ought to be possible: cultural regulations are less confining and work is more various. No longer are there only a few activities and professions for the majority of us. Now too, men are not alone in an interest in sexual fulfillment. Well bred women are more likely to have the capacity and interest to be sexually fulfilling; yet new problems have arisen.

The separate pulls of careers is one. Men and women now have the possibility of careers that pull them frequently apart. Apart, in sexually deprived states, they meet others who are eager to love them, or have sex with them. In our sexually stimulating and relatively free society, these happenstance arrangements frequently attack and tempt the best relationships.

And when we have found the supremely interesting one, the apple of our eye, the person who will make our life different, the fulfillment of all our hopes and dreams, are we going to let them free? Thus value paralyzes us and makes us the jailers of our lovers. It helps if we believe that we too have value in their eyes, and that they will come back to us.

To keep our love going we must avoid three primary dangers: holding our tongue out of fear of loss, holding on too tightly out of fear of loss, staying too long on our island together to the exclusion of the world. These are the principal destroyers of a good love relationship.

Love as an Addiction

Beginning love is so pleasureable, there are many who suffer from excessively valuing the activity. Love addicts, they are called by some. I hear the men more often called compulsive lovers. Dreamers, wanderers, livers in fantasyland they're called. They have learned the pleasures of falling in love, and do it repeatedly. They prefer a succession of happy beginnings to the struggle of an ongoing relationship. They either lie to others, or to themselves, to keep their excitement going with each new possibility.

Here the problem is one of *affirmation*. Few areas provide as many easy opportunities for praise, statements of worth and endearment as love. The good feeling we get as we "fall in love" once more competes handily with the pleasures of heroin. Some addicts choose one, some the other. The love addict can repeatedly gain the good feeling from being told he is wonderful, planning a new and glorious life, looking forward to a home with his beloved. For many reasonably attractive young people it is easier to to start a new relationship than to get a degree, a promotion on the job, or paint a picture. The adventure once available in migration to new lands is not available to most of us. Exploring sexual relationships has become the new unknown land that beckons and absorbs us. Perhaps this new person will really treat us specially despite our faults. They may know something about love making unknown to help us to overcome our armor and stiffness, and lead us to new delights and intimacies.

16
Selfishness and Love

A South-African witch doctor, when asked what was the most important thing he had to say or do for his followers recently, replied, "Tell them to stop thinking about themselves all the time and do for other people." Preparing to write this chapter, I was realizing that my most steadfast friends were those for whom I had first gone an extra mile, without calculation, out of love, gratuitously.

The needs of the self, and the needs of our significant others create different pulls upon us, which have often been discussed by the most poetic and brilliant psychological and ethical thinkers. Clarifying the conflicting solutions to this polarity will allow you to be clearer in your thinking, your planning, and your choices.

Are Relationships Necessary?

What we are dealing with here is fundamentally two questions. First, are relationships necessary? Are they in man's best interest? Will a person live better, have more, be happier, accomplish more, with relationships, or without them? The answer to this question is apparently obvious to some people, not others.

What is the best strategy to make them work, when and if they are desireable. A "relationship" is generally marked by two things: first an expectation of mutual aid or joint activity: partnership, tennis, love, child-raising conversation, intimacy, help, sex; and second by a lack of precise and immediate calculation. To buy groceries is not to be in a relationship. Only after some regular conversation beyond an exact and measured exchange of hellos begins, is a relationship there. Going to a prostitute sex is provided; but the exchange is too exact for it to be relational in nature. Often the prostitute struggles to keep the transaction limited and commercial while the customer struggles to make it more amorphous, outside the precisely measured, a relationship.

On the side of having relationships is the fact that most important human activities cannot be done alone. While mountain climbing is seen as the triumph of man over nature, this individualistic activity is really a co-operative one: it requires a whole team to get one or two men to the top. Similarly for other activities of any substance or challenge, more than one person is required. On the negative side is the fact that some people become embittered and choose to limit their relationships with age. Howard Hughes was not alone in choosing to withdraw from the world to a darkened and drug filled room. Other rich men make similar choices once their need to co-operate with others for business purposes has passed.

While some sex machines and pleasure devices have been developed, no real technologically sophisticated approach has yet been funded. What would happen I wonder if Procter and Gamble, MGM, or Apple computer put its energy into developing sexual pleasure devices, and making them socially acceptable with the help of advertising?

A patient of mine, sad over his most recent failed relationship, got tired of his loneliness. He thought his was sexual deprivation and picked up a partner suitable only for the briefest sexual encounter. "I felt just as lonely afterwards. I was at exactly the same lonely spot twenty minutes later." Part of the need for relationships comes from our need for connectedness and security. We need to be part of the world in some way, know that we can rely on it in pain or in danger. We can't totally live our lives with carefully measured transactions for mutual advantage.

Love relationships, combining physical, intellectual and emotional intimacy are the easiest way for many to feel connected. Other alliances are possible. The military encourages a buddy system in battle. Being part of a religious order or a revolutionary party seems to provide both safety, connectedness, and participation for some few in our time. In other times and places, that has been a more widespread choice. (Strikingly, 40 per cent of the males of Mongolia were Buddhist monks at the beginning of the 20th century.)

Selfish or Self-centered

Certainly, enduring relationships are impossible with a selfish attitude. Says the Oxford Dictionary: "Selfish: devoted to or concerned with one's own advantage or welfare to the exclusion of regard for others." Practically by definition, selfishness makes relationships impossible with people who have a modicum of self respect or self-worth, at least after the selfishness is discovered. One always feels a great sense of deprivation around the selfish. They seem not to have learned to expect anything good from other people for more than ten minutes. They need to get what they can, right away. One can understand selfishness as a sense of despair about human relationships. In a way, the selfish person lives by the motto, "Let thine own self be enough."

The other-centered stance is much less common in the generations since WWII. The extreme form of this position is martyrdom, but it can have its rational side. The motto of the other-centered is, "Make others strong and happy, and they will take care of you in return." Usually the other-centered person is not clearly seen as making a bargain. Often the object of her concern simply comes to expect her offerings as what she says they are: gifts with no obligations. In another way their need and deviousness is known. Their apparent lack of desire for reciprocity sometimes breeds contempt and a perverse sort of pleasure in cheating them on the part of more aggressive persons. Frequently they end up as doormats.

Having versus Being

Self-centeredness is an important idea that has been used in two different ways. It's most common usage today is somewhat similar to selfish: a person who is always aware of his need to "have"; someone who calculates his interests like a businessman. This person differs from the selfish person however in being less grasping, and with a better sense of his long-term interests in being on good terms with others. Self centered has an older meaning: a recognition that the heart and soul of a person requires the cultivation of certain kinds of productivity and virtue in order to "be" a person. This kind of self-centeredness focuses on the "being" of a person, instead of his "having."

Being self-centered still leaves open the question of what are the important needs the your "self" has from a relationship. Being in an exploitative relationship is not a long term solution. Oppressors find their human qualities destroyed also. Those they oppress and exploit will give them only what can be extracted. Being self centered, in its best and oldest sense, means creating a relational world of trust, friendship, and mutual regard, where love and productivity can flourish.

While self-centered people who are in the "having" mode often recognize the importance of other people in their life, they tend to look at relationships with their needs to "have more" as the central focus. The hope of this self-centered standpoint is to be in an intimate relationship as a way to have more love, time with another, more sex, and other "things" that only a "relationship" can produce. Unfortunately, it seems hard for two self-centered people in the having mode to do that easily. There is a constant struggle to see around whose center the relationship revolves, a desperation about who will get more from the arrangement. Often the relationship can only stay static, since doing something new will involve a struggle over who gets the important new energy. The tendency for this kind of self-centered person, relating to his twin, self-centered person, is to become increasingly autonomous and separate. As a result, the relationship becomes increasingly thin, and vulnerable to more intense involvements that promise more. In practical terms what is needed is a more relational stance, an attitude that puts some emphasis on maintaining a healthy relational environment.

The current focus on self-centered relationships is a reaction against the old values which were community and relationship oriented. Women especially have felt ripped off from being in relationships where men seem to have gotten the goods: status, prestige, free time, relatively easy or interesting jobs, someone to help them. Many women, and some men, were relationship and community oriented to the point of martyrdom and self-obliteration. While this is still true for some people, the current cultural problem is just the opposite. There is a great problem in making relationships work, period, for any protracted time. The number of single people is rapidly increasing. Relationships are thin and superficial. Builders are designing houses for unrelated strangers.

There is an alertness, a fear of giving oneself away

in a committed relationship that borders on paranoia. Many people have learned how to say "no" to entanglements but in the process, they have lost the ability to create much in their personal life. They don't have the freedom to say "yes" to some fulfilling personal arrangement in their life. The problem is atomization. Society is tending to break down to its smallest units. Of course there remains the hope that this will lead to new and better combinations, more suitable to contemporary life. So far, all alternatives to the family, however, are showing themselves to be insubstanial, and are not even attracting much in the way of stray atoms.

Revolt Against Community and Family

While homosexuality has a variety of psychological roots, in part its current rise can be seen as a revolution against the family, as well as against specific sex roles. In certain urban areas, a large minority of homosexuals coexist with heterosexuals who have chosen a single life, or a life of relatively transient relationships, or a life without the restrictions of family. In San Francisco itself, the majority of inhabitants are single, a new statistic in urban America. Single life has taken on many of the sexual characteristics that were once the exclusive preserve of homosexual life: transience, passionate hope, despair, and childlessness.

The current cancerous growth of the megalopolis contributes to the minimization of community feeling. The separation between the homes of fellow workers and friends makes casual community life almost impossible. Distance makes being with friends a sacrifice. There is little understanding that such altruism preserves a community for all. While many self-centered people, as opposed to selfish people, understand the needs of others, their constant referral back to themselves often makes it hard for them to be fully invested in their relationships. Sometimes they are bright enough to see this and change, rescuing a failing relationship.

Thus Barbara, an energetic and vivacious wife, seemed happy enough with her marriage while her somewhat older husband, Bill, put her through art school. The art students she met, while somewhat flirtatious, were no serious temptation for her, as long as her husband was home every night.

A promotion to supervising accountant put him into travelling, sometimes for weeks at a time. Barbara wasn't about to be sexually and emotionally deprived. She simply began to have an affair. Her affairs lasted for several years, one after another, until her husband confronted her with his realization that she was often sexually involved. Fortunately, he faced the issue from a feeling standpoint instead of from a punitive one. Bill let Barbara know his pain over her affairs, and indicated that he would pursue his own on an experimental basis. He was less interested in other love affairs than she.

This state of affairs lasted for a short time. Barbara wanted a child and realized that she had to give up her affairs if she wanted Bill to invest himself into creating a family with her. With some regret about the loss of sexual goodies, she put her energy back into her marriage, putting off the eventual resolution of her interest in other men until her child was more grown.

Sometimes we need to put ourselves first, at other moments the needs of the relationship require us to submerge ourselves to the requirements of the other. Theoretically two self-centered people ought to be able to create more by taking turns helping each other. In fact, this often doesn't occur. The constant preoccupation with being sure to get the best deal for one's self, with "having more," often interferes with either party getting what they want.

I suspect that the problem lies in the roots of being self-centered in the having mode. Being self-centered is most likely a relatively rational and mature reaction to disappointment. Given such a history, it is no wonder self centered people tend to be very vigilant about any lessening of their "fair and equal" share.

Much of our institutional life is being corroded by excessive calculation of self-interest. The idea of sacrificing self to comunity has little currency: as a result, the community is collapsing. Why take time to vote, when your vote counts only a little, and your time is valuable? Why fight in a war, and run the chance of death when someone else might do your fighting for you? You can survive and enjoy the fruits of victory.

Some scholars have argued that we have mistakenly introduced the ethics and methods of business into personal relationships, thereby destroying them. The captain of a robber band argues thusly in a French novel from the late 18th century, at the dawn of business civilization:

> "...If I came across a traveller, a victim, and the traveller had only one penny, I ought to kill him for that. For even one penny can be of value to me and someone else's life is just that, someone else's. Of what value is his life to me? Nothing!"

In the United States recently, greed has affected relationships in the experience area. We have wanted more experientially, being largely free from material want for forty years, and even from the fear of want until very recently. We have been secure in our ability to start over; even if not on a physical frontier. We can try a new job, a new school, a new wife. Our options remain open. This state of affairs is changing. While the traditional, bound-in relationships are no longer attractive, neither are casual affairs or thin, primarily sexual relationships. Perhaps some Buddhist saint can move through life without attachments, taking what he needs wherever he finds it. The rest of mankind needs hope and security and can feel disappointment. To those, this book has been addressed. Build your relationship with security for both of you, while recognizing that the possibility of a voluntary dissolution, a termination, is there. Create a world for each of you that allows productivity and being in the world.

A powerful song of the sixties dealt with the tremendous fluidity of relationships as people broke free of their traditional bonds. Janis Joplin sang "Get It While You Can," contending with this situation, and then killed herself in a motel room. Most of us need some security. Perhaps "Hold On, But Not Too Tightly," needs to be our current song.

We need to live with the fact that most people are less committed to a particular relationship than in the past, and be prepared to renegotiate our relationships every two or three years—towards a new form or to dissolution.

Choice is important. Relationships are not a one person game. Choose to be in a relationship with someone who is willing to make the relationship important, and communicate when it is not. Take that attitude also, and you may expect a more fulfilled and satisfied life.

To accomplish this, remember to stay focused on your own needs. See if you can do this without getting greedy, without seeing the other person as a resource to exploit. Don't blame the other for your not having what you want, but hang in for a while and struggle a bit to work at least part of it out. Do you criticize the others' character when they don't automatically give you what you want? Try telling them your needs instead. Be helpful to them when they say what their wishes are, but don't let them push you around. Combine knowing yourself, and your own needs, which is the theme of this book, with being sensitive to the needs of others. Remember that a relationship is not like buying a car, there must be a trusting world created that seems to both parties a place worth preserving. Building such a world gives your relationship the best chance to survive time and changes in individual needs.